Centre of
Excellence for
Social Learning

How to Take Your School on a Journey to Outstanding:

five building blocks to maximise
children's social learning potential

Sam Frankel

John Fowler

Foreword by Baroness Massey of Darwen

Promoting Transformation in Education

First published in 2016
by EquippingKids
Old Post Office, Wall Under Heywood, Church Stretton,
Shropshire, SY6 7DU, UK

www.equippingkids.org

for and on behalf of the
Centre of Excellence for Social Learning

www.sociallearning.org

British Library Cataloguing in Publication Data
A CIP catalogue record for this book is available from the British Library

ISBN 978-0-9558020-1-0

Printed and bound in Great Britain by
Witley Press Ltd 24-26 Greevegate, Hunstanton PE36 6AD
www.witleypress.co.uk

To all those children and teachers who have been part of this journey.

We write this in the hope of encouraging all those connected to schools of the value of education to make a difference.

Contents

Acknowledgements

We have worked with so many children and adults to formulate these ideas that it would be impossible to name them all. We do, however, recognise their impact and thank them for their patience and encouragement, as we have tested and explored our thoughts. It is important to note that children have been at the centre of the ideas that we have developed in this work and we thank them for the challenges, the fun, the insight and the creativity that they have provided.

With special thanks to Esther Hamilton, Hannah Trickett and Steve Emmett in the UK for their role in not only piloting these ideas, but also for reading drafts of this work. In Canada, thanks to Sally McNamme and particularly to Pat Dunne for his encouragement and advice. Thanks to friends and family for the comments on drafts and thanks to the students on the Childhood and Social Institutions programme at Kings at Western University, Canada for their enthusiastic engagement in highlighting the importance of sharing these ideas.

Foreword

Schools cannot solve all the problems of society. What they can do is foster an environment for 'social learning' which benefits pupils, teachers and the school community.

The *social learning agenda* proposed in this book enables pupils to gain, and practise, skills of communication and to develop positive relationships. It encourages behaviour which is sensitive and resilient to life in school and beyond school. It encourages self esteem and the confidence to influence the world of school and the world outside.

Academic achievement is, of course, important. Research and anecdotal evidence from schools shows that social skills can support and enhance academic success.

Through practical and clear steps, this book encourages educators to reassess ways in which they can be part of establishing a learning environment which gives children the opportunity to develop and expand skills for life.

Doreen E Massey
(Baroness Massey of Darwen)

Introductions

What makes school special?

We believe it is the potential of education to make a difference to children's lives!

Do you believe it?

Teaching stands out as a career that people pursue because of a set of ideals, a belief that they can be part of making *that* difference. It is a mindset that offers exciting possibilities, but the only trouble is that the reality of the day to day means that this ideal gets side-tracked, put on hold or indeed forgotten altogether. So many teachers leave the profession before they have even really got started. So what of those ideals that took them there in the first place?

In this book we want to share a model with you that we believe puts those involved in school very much back in the business of making a difference to children's lives. We have called this the *social learning agenda*. It is a concept that we have tried and tested and have seen work, so now we want to share it with you. As you read, we will mix some theory and practice as we present five building blocks that can bring about change in your school.

Each school is very different, every class is very different, each teacher is different and so too is every child, so what works in one school might not necessarily work in another. Therefore, although the principles underlying our model are common and agreed, how the model comes to be applied may look different. This means that as you read and engage in the ideas and case studies, you will need to draw out those aspects that are going to be most relevant to you, as you translate the principles into practice for children (and adults) connected with your school.

This book is aimed at anyone interested in education. From the professional, to the parent, to the policy maker and student, this book is for those who want to get excited about the impact that education really can have in children's lives. It is, however, head teachers, classroom teachers and support staff, who are going to be in a position to use these techniques most directly. We, therefore, have tried to set this book out such that it makes it easy for the busy practitioner to engage in the ideas and then to put them into practice.

Introducing the schools

We have used five case study schools to help illustrate the ideas within this book. Each of these schools has influenced our ideas as we engaged with the different characteristics of these unique learning communities. Although we refer to certain schools more in this work, due to their relevance in introducing the *social learning agenda*, all have had an impact and future work will make use of the growing data that is being collected from these and other schools. The schools are:

Parent Power - School 1: An upper middle class school, where aspirations were driven to a significant extent by the power of the parents. It was a school that saw a team start to establish ideas and ways of engaging children that would form part of the model which we were to create some years later. An outstanding school that showed us that if we get the model right it can have significant results.

Time for Change - School 2: An ethnically diverse community with a significant degree of economic hardship. A school that was a concern for the educational authorities for many years and was at the very bottom of the league tables. A traditional approach had been repeatedly tried but was not working. It was in this school that we developed our *social learning agenda* in concentrated research projects developed over a number of years.

Keen and Eager - School 3: A mainly white working class community where a new head teacher provided an energy and passion to drive up standards and expectations, supported by a strong team. From the start, the *social learning agenda* became a tool that was used as part of this process. It was the first school to fully adopt our Social Learning Model.

Slow and Steady - School 4: A nursery and infant school in a middle-class community. The staff had lots of good ideas but were in need of a framework to give them some consistency and direction. They are using the *social learning agenda* to give that focus.

A Way Forward - School 5: A mainly white working class community, where a new and inexperienced (yet enthusiastic) headteacher was looking for an effective framework to help drive the strategic development of the school. The *social learning agenda* enabled the staff to agree upon the focus of the school, helped translate their vision into a meaningful 'language' and provided a framework for school-based initiatives.

These ideas are being developed within primary schools, although they will also have application for secondary education, further and higher education, we have yet to trial them in these arenas.

Introducing us

As well as introducing the schools, we also thought it might be worth letting you know who we are. The reason for this is that we are both going to be offering contributions to this book that reflect our background and experiences. As mentioned already, our ideas for the *social learning agenda* have taken a number of years to evolve into what they are today. These ideas merge a unique blend of professional teaching experience and creative practices with research and academic expertise. It is a view that seeks to further our ambition to see academic research better inform classroom practice, and classroom practice to better inform academic research, all with the aim of improving outcomes for children.

As we write, therefore, we thought it might be helpful to let you know whose voice lies behind the text that you are reading.

Dr Sam Frankel: We are going to start with me, for the simple reason that most of the text you will read will be in this font and I am the one writing it. That being said my voice in this text reflects not only my views but all I have learnt from working with John and, therefore, it must be seen as bringing together the combined ideas that sit behind the *social learning agenda*.

As I write this book, it has literally been 20 years since I started working with children. I remember well those early days as a lifeguard and swimming teacher, shivering in the pool as five and six year olds splashed away trying to accomplish their first width without their armbands. Being part of that individual achievement, which meant so much to those young swimmers, certainly influenced my efforts to set up and run a children's educational charity as well as my passion for teaching and writing about children (both in the UK and beyond). Throughout I have been driven by a real desire to understand children's worlds and to be part of equipping them with knowledge and skills to make the most of their potential.

I have been very fortunate that I have managed to carve out a path that has allowed me to sit outside of traditional careers as I have combined both a practical and academic interest in children's role in society. I have been fortunate to work with children in schools across the UK with educational charity Act 4. Over the last ten years it has allowed me to work with over 65,000 mainly primary aged children, as we develop creative value based programmes. I am an Honorary Research Fellow at the University of Sheffield and have recently been in Canada as a Visiting Professor at Kings at Western University, Ontario, where I was given the opportunity to, amongst other things, consider the application of our *social learning agenda* in a North American context. This transatlantic dialogue has reminded me how much we can learn from each other as we seek to find ways of furthering children's school experience. The Social Learning project has been so exciting as it brings together theory and practice and offers a practical framework that has had a positive impact on children's everyday lives.

John Fowler: From the rather traditional font Sam is using - I have chosen 'chalkboard' to reflect the fact that I have spent my career teaching in schools. I have 30 years experience in education during which I have had a number of roles; as a head teacher, an Ofsted Registered Inspector, a Local Authority Advisor, notably leading a 'teaching and learning' team and a Leadership Development Partner. I have advised schools, here in the UK and overseas, local authorities and national organisations on 'leading learning schools', as well as continuing to offer independent advice.

For many years I have been involved with ideas around 'learning to learn'; as part of this I was a founding member of a Teaching and Learning Alliance, and have shared my ideas to a range of forums to further such debate. Sam and I (with colleagues from some of the schools we work with) spoke at the House of Lords on promoting children's well being and I am actively involved in the National Children's Bureau.

I aim to support schools in 'developing and making explicit their school's ethos', stimulating and leading change, developing a language for learning across the school, turning declared intentions into effective practice and finally developing a community of learners that involves, all children and their families, all staff and governors and where possible, the wider community. I like a challenge!

Other useful information

International Readers: if you are reading this book in a country outside of the English education system then you will realise pretty quickly some of the differences in terminology. Although I think you will make sense of this with ease, the only aspect that might be of value at the start is a guide that matches ages with the different year groups used in schools.

Early Years Foundation Stage (EYFS) - below 5 years (children can start in a reception class at the age of 4 years).

Key Stage 1
    Year 1: 5-6 years
    Year 2: 6-7 years

Key Stage 2
    Year 3: 7-8 years
    Year 4: 8-9 years
    Year 5: 9-10 years
    Year 6: 10-11 years

References: In order to make the text that follows as easy to read as possible, we have been understated in the number of citations that we have included in the text. Key ideas that shape the arguments are cited, however if you would like any further information then please get in touch.

Contacting us: Through this book we aim to promote dialogue. We would, therefore, be very keen to hear from you. If you have thoughts, ideas, comments, case studies or questions then please contact us - ask@sociallearners.org

We will be supporting this work with a web site which will help to offer a platform to promote this dialogue and to further, what we hope, will be a shared ambition for transforming children's experience of education through embracing our *social learning agenda* - **www.sociallearners.org**

The journey begins: children & learning

It was around 2006 that I first walked into a school led by John (Parent Power - School 1). At the time I was working regularly in many schools, but as soon as I walked in, I felt there was something different here. It was not the welcome by the staff in the reception, it was not the displays on the wall, or the fish tank in the corridor, it was not the boxes of this and that piled to one side in the hall. It was the children.

So what was it about these children that made them different? There was purpose in their walk and a confidence in their greetings. It was as if I had entered, what I have imagined it is like in the offices of those fabled Californian technology giants, where everyone feels motivated by the goals and are passionate about ensuring that their part in the bigger project is completed to the best of their ability. You sensed a hunger to pursue the next task and an excitement about what they might discover. In short there was an overwhelming desire to learn.

For many years I had been pursuing some academic ideas around power and the extent to which learning is more effective when it takes place in an atmosphere of partnership. Here it was in practice. The children were partners, respected for who they were, not for what they might become. They were important, first and foremost, as individuals.

A few years later I received an e-mail from John. John had moved to a new school (Time for Change - School 2) and he was inviting me to come in and see whether there was anything I might be able to bring to their developing social, personal and moral curriculum. This new school was very different. In fact, it could not have been more different. From the prosperity of a leafy commuter village to an area of significant deprivation these schools were different in every way, culturally, economically, socially. Not only that, but it was a move from a school that was 'outstanding' (the highest result offered by the national inspection body Ofsted) to one that had been of great concern to the Local Education Authority for many years, gaining notoriety by finding itself at the very bottom of the county league tables.

So it was with great interest that I drove over to see the new school and most particularly, the children. What were they going to be like, would there be that sense of partnership? After a few phone calls to find out exactly where in the maze of roads and houses that made up the estate the school was, I arrived. Outside everything was most certainly different. But inside...

I met John, walked down one corridor and another. We visited one, two, three classrooms. Yes, it was there again. That motivation to learn, together. It was not as strong, not as defined as before but something was going on. The children clearly felt safe and keen to make the most of the opportunities that school offered. But there was a hesitancy, an uncertainty that seemed to hover all around, there was a lack of confidence.

JF: When I arrived in Time for Change - School 2, I found a school that was not sure what it was or why it was there. The children really had no idea of their place or purpose (nor in fact did the staff). The result was nothing short of chaos. Children were climbing on top of the cupboards, standing on desks, and I constantly feared that at any second I would be called on to break up a fight, the situation was as bad as I think it could have been. At every level the school was lost. Attendance was terrible, attainment was low. So where do you start? I decided I needed to start everywhere, which included a focus on:

- Promoting positive attitudes towards learning
- Raising self esteem for children, pupils and parents
- Shifting a culture in which both staff and children felt 'done unto'
- To instil a purpose to school which everyone could buy into

It may sound a bit like a wish list in a school that was so troubled. At the centre of this lay the challenge of breaking down a range of assumptions that had effectively created a wall between the children and staff within the school as well as the parents outside. It was a desire to bring these groups together behind a shared passion for learning that had to be our drive. Thus with the support of key members of staff, we set about finding ways to get these walls knocked down, recognising that this might mean moving one brick at a time.

Any process of change is step by step and by the time I got involved, change was clearly happening. The way in which the children were engaged and participating seemed worlds away from how they were when John arrived. The children were smiling in the corridors, keen to say hello and to talk about what they were doing; they had recognised they had a role (although perhaps not yet exactly what that was) in this learning community. Whatever John and his team were doing was altering the way in which the children were able to engage with their learning. However, as I chatted with John, his team and the children it became clear that it was hard to define exactly what it was that was creating this change. Literally overnight John and I realised that if we could start to make visible those processes that were taking place, if we could identify, capture, enhance, develop and share them, then maybe we could find a formula to boost that confidence in both children and staff that would really mark this journey of transformation.

JF: It takes '1000 days to transform a school' suggests the academic Louise Stool and I think I would agree. Indeed it was three years after taking the job that we got that visit from the inspectors. The school was now in a very different place. Rather than heading out onto the playground wearing a mental 'flak jacket', I looked forward to hearing what the children had been doing as they queued up to tell me about their learning. I no longer sat nervously waiting for the next knock on the office door calling me to the latest incident; instead those knocks now offered a chance to look at a painting or a piece of writing as the children talked of their progress. Attendance was up and a considerable amount of my time was spent showing prospective parents around. This was new.

So it was with that usual sense of nervous excitement that we acknowledged the call that the inspectors were on their way. All I wanted was a recognition of the hard work the staff and children had put in. I knew attainment in the rigid format of the recoding process remained a challenge, although the children's progress was exceptional. As the inspectors left, it was with relief and delight that I was able to share with an emotional staff team that the school was not only reaching the standards required (we were 'good') but that in certain areas we were 'outstanding'.

The journey we took in 'Time to Change - School 2' gave us the chance to start defining the model, a model that has taken years of work and the involvement of many talented teachers and engaged children. It also offered us a starting point from which to begin to share these ideas with many more schools. As use of the *social learning agenda* has grown, so we have begun to realise how different each school's journey can be and how important it is that schools embrace the uniqueness of that journey, rather than seeking some pre-defined script for change.

So what you are about to embark on is your *own* journey, one that will be unique to you and your school, one that will have ups and downs and a number of wrong turns. However, we hope that what you find in the coming chapters will give you the confidence to take that journey. Nothing you read will have a negative effect on your school, but it may help you to discover new frontiers that allow the children you work with to make the most of their learning potential.

The social learning agenda

What is the point of school?

In his book *Dumbing Us Down* (2005) John Taylor Gatto, presents a scathing attack on the school system in the US. An award winning teacher himself, he says:

> With lessons like the ones I teach day after day it should be little wonder we have a real national crisis...young people are indifferent to almost everything except the diversion of toys and violence...[they] cannot concentrate on anything for long...they are mistrustful of intimacy...they hate solitude, are cruel, materialistic, dependent, passive, violent, timid... (Gatto, 2005:17)

The reason for this? The curriculum. Fundamentally, Gatto argues that school and the way in which the curriculum has evolved means that it defines the way children are taught such that we (society) are set up to fail and to continue to fail! What is needed is a fight to regain education, one in which children have time, time primarily to understand who they are in relation to all that is around them.

> Right now we are taking from our children all the time that they need to develop self-knowledge. That has to stop. We have to invent school experiences that give that time back. We need to trust children from a very early age with independent study, perhaps arranged in school, but which takes place away from the institutional setting. We need to invent curricula where each kid has a chance to develop private uniqueness and self reliance. (Gatto, 2005: 29ff)

So I ask again, what is the point of school?

Gatto is among others who are at present calling for a revolution in education. Who has failed to hear Sir Ken Robinson's blockbuster TED talks? If you have missed them, then this can be quickly remedied by searching 'www.ted.com'. In his 2010 presentation, he champions the potential of each child and challenges his audience to realise that evolution in education is not enough, for that is simply improving a model that is already broken, what is needed is 'something else'.

Our model argues that this 'something else' can come from re-considering the social dimension of children's educational experience. This is an obvious theme in both Gatto and Robinson's work as they highlight the importance of the individual and it is not new. It can be seen as a feature in 'democratic schools' such as Summerhill School in Suffolk, England or Sudbury Valley School, Massachusetts, US and in the ethos behind Steiner and Montessori education to name but two.

But what is it? Acknowledging a social dimension to learning is one thing, however, the problem for the practitioner is what does that really mean on a Tuesday afternoon in science or on a Friday morning in literacy, or indeed on any day of the week in the playground or lunch hall? In fact, when we really stop to think about it, how effective is the curriculum in allowing the practitioner to support the child to grow as an individual, one who has the skills required to be a lifelong learner?

JF: What is the point of school?

To a great extent for the most of us, national or more locally defined curriculums play a significant part in shaping how we come to think about our schools. Although we will argue later that we need to be more creative in how we see the curriculum, it does for so many of us offer a starting point. The problem is that not only do those who set the curriculums fear the social dimension of learning, they fear the idea of learning itself.

Let me give you an example, with the onset of the national curriculum, as a Local Authority Inspector I was part of a bid to undertake some developmental work focusing on Enquiry Skills in Geography. We involved teachers, developed a framework for action research, tested and evaluated classroom activities for teachers in Key Stage 1 and 2. When we submitted our thoughts and ideas we were informed that 'we had wandered too far into teaching and learning which was not the remit of the National

Curriculum Council'. My personal thoughts were that we had not casually wandered into teaching and learning, but in fact kept teaching and more importantly learning as a central part of the curriculum rather than being driven by curriculum content.

The reality of the situation that we have at the moment is that for the majority of teachers, we need to continue to work with the system. However, a starting point comes when we first question the curriculum and second, untangle ourselves from the belief that the curriculum must define the point of school. In fact, what if, the best way to reach those curriculum goals were to approach school differently, to centre it around a social dimension?

John Taylor Gatto's analysis at times appears quite gloomy. However, I firmly believe that those within schools have an element of control over their practices that allows them, whatever the agenda that sits above them, to reclaim education on behalf of the children that they teach. For this you need a focus and for us that means pinning down what we mean by this social dimension to learning. Our definition, therefore, offers a starting place, a basis on which one can reflect and react. Our *social learning agenda* says that the focus of the school community should not principally be about meeting government targets, whether in attainment or in terms of knowledge acquisition, although these remain important, rather the primary and constant focus must be on maximising the child's potential as a learner, and as a result meeting those ever changing targets. The focus of this agenda, must therefore be in establishing the 'social learner' by:

- Allowing the individual child to grow in their awareness of themselves and others.

- Equipping children with knowledge and skills so that they can successfully navigate the complexities of the social world they are part of.

- Providing a foundation to maximise the child's learning potential in school and to increase children's participation and engagement in their families and communities.

However, to allow the 'social learner' to flourish he or she needs to be supported by five pillars. Those pillars provide a learning community with five areas for attention and together these make up a *social learning agenda*. The pillars are:

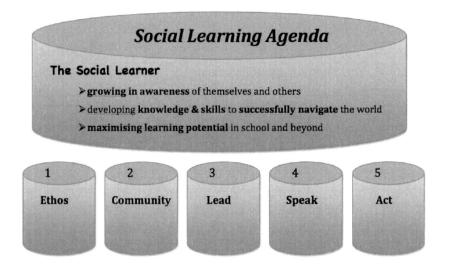

Ethos: establish children as partners
Community: design a space for the social learner
Lead: champion a learning process
Speak: compose a language for social engagement
Act: initiate opportunities for practice.

The following chapters will address each of these in turn, however it is important to note we are not suggesting that these are dealt with in a chronological order. Although 'ethos' has to be the starting point, the other areas can develop at different times and at different rates.

So what is the point of school? Our answer is that it is and has to be - the 'social learner'.

Now we know what we are working towards it is time to explore just what this means for you at your school.

A note:

Social Learning is a term that has been used by a number of academics. It is often associated with a psychological perspective as seen in the work of Albert Bandura. However, here, although we use the term 'social learning', our emphasis is on the active role that the child plays in this process of learning as they make meanings as a result of the social context and interactions that they are part of. This reflects an important difference to those original ideas. For rather than social learning being linked to the 'conditioning' or 'imitation' of a passive child, as these earlier theories suggest, for us the child is seen as skilled and competent in their assessment of the social world around them. It is this capacity for engaging with society that sees children involved in the subtleties of negotiating the social world, as they make strategic decisions, which shape their actions in response to the context they find themselves in (our theoretical position is developed in the following chapter). It is only by recognising *this* active social dimension, both in relation to the individual and to learning itself, that one can truly explore children's learning potential (whether in terms of reaching attainment targets, or simply in developing the skills for ongoing collaboration and research, with implications that stretch far beyond a classroom).

Why not use another term to avoid confusion? Good question. The reason for this is that to talk about what we do as social learning, is exactly what it is, we are, therefore, very happy to create an ownership dispute over this term, because in our context there is simply no better way to describe it, as we focus on the power of the 'social' in shaping the journey of the learner.

Creating Change:

- What are you thinking at the moment; is there personal accord or discord with what you have read so far?
- How would you currently define 'social learning'?
- What impact do you think the *social learning agenda* could have in your situation?

Building block 1 – *ethos*: establish children as partners

Introduction

	Social Learning Aims	Pillar One: Ethos	Principles or Drivers
The Social Learner	Allowing the individual child to grow in their awareness of themselves and others. Equipping children with knowledge and skills so that they can successfully navigate the complexities of the social world they are part of. Providing a foundation to maximise the child's learning potential in school and to increase children's participation and engagement in their families and communities.	Ethos: establish children as partners	Engaging with the child as a social agent (a competent meaning maker)
			Recognition of the child in the context of *their* social world
			An overriding ambition to promote social knowledge and skills as the objective of learning
			Practice that reflects children's learning through active and informed engagement with the individual
			A commitment to relationships that value the child and nurture mutual respect

Ethos has to be the starting place.

As John showed me around his new school (Time for Change - School 2), that first time, he kept repeating, "it would have been very different if you had been here a year ago". In one classroom, to the backdrop of that gentle chatter that accompanies children focused on a learning task, he told me that if we had been standing in this same room a year ago children would be literally climbing desks and throwing chairs, and almost hanging off the ceilings. Then (as discussed earlier) children and staff saw school very differently with the result that what was taking place in the classroom was a long way from any idea of effective learning.

A shared purpose for both adults (all staff and parents) and children must be key to effective learning. However, establishing a shared vision within the classroom can only start by recognising the need for this to be a partnership between children and adults. What do we mean by partnership? We mean a common goal and for all members of that learning community to understand their role and to be active in pursuing it.

JF: Time to Change - School 2 was beset by many years of children and staff having:

- Low expectations
- Limited aspirations
- A lack of value or sense of importance

The Local Education Authority wanted a quick fix which they had pursued for a number of years by employing little more than a carrot and stick approach. This saw the focus on teachers setting an agenda which children and parents simply had to follow. It was an article on self-regulated learning that for me offered a different place to start. What this article suggested was that children needed to be allowed to take some responsibility and ownership for their learning. It challenged the view that staff alone were responsible for the children's journey in school and rather it suggested that staff needed to be working more closely with children to allow them to take more responsibility for their own learning. For 'Time to Change - School 2' it announced a move towards a partnership in learning, one that aimed to put back all that had been missing.

Our starting place, therefore, as we introduce the *social leaning agenda* to you has to be the need for all parties involved in school to consider or re-consider individual expectations and attitudes towards their roles, their relationships and their understandings of one another.

This applies to you! Yes, whether you have been involved in school for a long time or a short time, these questions are ones that we should continually be asking ourselves as we challenge and reassess our attitudes and understandings. An obvious time to do this are those times of change, at the start of the school year, or if new members or groups join a class, although we should not feel these are the only times. We need to make sure that we are not consumed by dominant discourses and ways of thinking about childhood that go against that invitation for partnership. All schools, to different extents are having to manage assumptions about children, which will affect the way that children come to be positioned in relation to adults. These assumptions have implications for the learning process and without engaging with them, our social learning journey will never even leave the car park!

In this chapter we are going to have to grapple with some of the theoretical 'stuff' but I think it is worth it, because if we are going to be part of setting in train a lasting process of change then we need to make sure we have got the foundations right before we start to build.

So here goes!

Recognising assumptions

JF: We all make assumptions and I must admit that schools and those of us involved in them are particularly prone to this. It is right that we challenge our use of those assumptions and the way they come to shape the perceptions we have of the children, and as a result affecting the way they come to see us. Fortunately, I have a constant reminder hanging in my home. It is one of those pictures that a child has drawn you that you know from first seeing it that you are never going to be able to throw it away.

To Mr Fowler

The picture is a portrait of me done by a 6 year old from a school early in my career as a head. There I am, moustache, tall but with the biggest nostrils you have ever seen (and my nose is not THAT big). An artistic mistake? No of course not, for that was exactly how the child saw me! As he was seated in the front row of the assembly hall, there I was standing in front of him, and as he looked up what he saw was my nose!

A few years later I read an article called *Maverick Heads (Hoy Group 2002)*, it highlighted that need for schools to continually question assumptions. It challenged headteachers to push boundaries and 'cross the line', taking on those areas of misunderstanding that had limited children's place in the learning environment for too long.

So what are these assumptions and how might they be impacting your school?

It is a level of awareness that is important here. For assumptions will always form a part of the way in which adults engage with children. However, too often assumptions can have a negative impact, limiting our perception of the child's potential and his or her capacity as a learner.

So who carries these assumptions, where do these assumptions come from and what do they look like? The first two parts of the question are in many ways interlinked. The way we as individuals come to understand children does, of course, stem from many sources. These sources reflect our own childhoods, how we were parented and how we were taught. It may reflect our professional journeys, the courses we have done and our practical experience of working with children in schools. All this takes place within a particular cultural context, where society's thinking about children, presented by the media, politicians and more, will influence us personally, within our peer groups and within the institutions within which we work.

A body of academic literature, which formally announced itself at the start of the 1990's, has promoted the idea that childhood is a social construction, with societies creating particular representations of the child that come to impact on both policy and practice. Significantly, the representations of children that emerge as dominant in our thinking today, reflect views that rely more on the way adults have come to understand children rather than from knowledge of the individual child themselves. As a result, children remain the objects of adult concerns. These dominant attitudes that draw on history, come to drive so much of how we think and act towards children as our knowledge reflects that desire to make sense of children as a universal group, whose competence is limited.

In school, this creates a cocktail of understandings that come together through us as individuals but which are also invariably shaped by the institution of school, its historical legacy and the expectations placed on it by policy makers, parents, inspectors and more. These understandings draw off these socially constructed ways of viewing the child, these dominant attitudes that are built on adult perceptions of childhood, rather than efforts by adults to develop their knowledge of children from and with the individual child themselves. This is the point. For it means that our knowledge of children reflects adult perception and not reality. The result is that throughout society, including in our schools, we come to engage with children on a false premise, a poor foundation, one that leads to misunderstanding and misdirection and which only serves to create barriers between children and adults, with implications for the potential of the individual child as a learner.

The impact of assumptions

The opening to Antoine de Saint Expurey's (1943) classic story *The Little Prince* highlights how, sometimes as adults, we can really miss the point. The narrator explains how at six years old he saw a book '*true stories from nature*', which inspired him to draw a picture. It showed a boa constrictor eating an elephant. This was clear to him and offered a frightening prospect, but from the limited perspective of the adult, they only saw a hat and as a result were not frightened at all. So he drew another picture (you can see these pictures by searching online) showing the elephant inside the boa constrictor but when he showed this to the adults their advice was 'to lay aside my drawings of boa constrictors, whether from the inside or outside and devote myself instead to geography, history, arithmetic, and grammar' (p6). The result of these adult comments for this six year old narrator were catastrophic,

> 'that is why at the age of six, I gave up what might have been a magnificent career as a painter. I had been disheartened by the failure of my Drawing Number One and my Drawing Number Two. Grown-ups never understand anything by themselves, and it is tiresome for children to be always and forever explaining things to them' (p6).

This literary example so clearly illustrates the way in which adult understandings can dominate and shape children's experiences. It contrasts with an example shared by Ken Robinson's 2006 TED talk, where he tells the story of the internationally renowned dancer and choreographer Dame Gillian Lynne whose need and potential as a child who wanted to dance were recognised and encouraged by adults, leading to a glittering career. Notably one that would never have come about had adults interpreted her inability to stay still in the classroom as a condition that just needed to be controlled.

The way we think about children shapes how we act towards them, defining the practices that we follow.

Example from Research: attitudes shaping practice

One example of this can be seen in the work of academic Paul Connolly (1998). He observed teachers working in an inner city school and looked at the way in which race and gender came to impact children's experiences of schools. A defining aspect of this research are Connolly's findings in relation to black boys. Black boys in this school were labelled with a set of adult assumptions. Those assumptions related to their behaviour and consequently to their capacity to be effective learners. One of the implications of adult perceptions was that the actions of black boys were responded to by staff with much harsher disciplinary techniques than that experienced by other children. It created a cycle in which the boys internalised those assumptions as they came to be reflected in their sense of identity.

> What I want to suggest…is that teacher pupil and pupil-pupil relations form a complex feed-back cycle where the actions of each tend to influence and exacerbate the other. In this sense it could be argued that the over-disciplining of Black boys tends to construct an image of them, among their peers, as being 'bad' and quintessentially masculine. This in turn, provides the context where Black boys are more likely to be verbally and physically attacked. As a consequence, Black boys are more likely to be drawn into fights and to develop 'hardened' identities, which then means they are more likely to be noticed by teachers and disciplined for being aggressive. The cycle is thus complete. (Connolly, 1998: 114).

What Connolly's work shows is that it was not an 'understanding of the child' that drove the way in which the adults in this school dealt with these children, but rather assumptions that reflected a broader perception of expected behaviour that were framed by race.

It has been and continues to be assumptions about children that affect so much of children's experience of school at every level, from interaction with mid-day supervisors to the work they do in class, to the tests that they are set by the government of the day.

Example from Research: children in school = a project

Berry Mayall (1994) provides a useful summary of these assumptions in relation to school, which reflect elements of these constructed views of childhood which are so influential. Although these views were shared 20 years ago, what is significant is that they are still as relevant to the debate around children in schools today. Under the heading 'contextual factors influencing learning and behaviour' (Mayall, 1994: 125) Mayall, in thinking about schools, lists:

- Socialisation as prescription
- Adult authority in context of institutional norms
- Adult construction of child as project
- Child construction of self as object

(ibid)

It is a perspective that sees school shaped by the way in which adults come to think about the child, rather than based on the way in which children think. It is therefore a model that reflects adult assumptions about childhood, rather than reflecting an understanding of children themselves.

The views expressed in these research examples reflect wider held views of the role and purpose of adults to mould, shape and define children's journey through childhood so that they might become a useful adult at the end of it. The child is a project, which is most effectively managed by adults establishing control and reinforcing this through systems that demonstrate their superior power. It is an approach which encourages a 'we know best' attitude and which ultimately drives a divide between children and adults, with a significant impact on the potential for learning. Recently this has come to be exemplified in an outcomes driven approach which seems to only value academic performance in the core subjects. The assumptions that support this approach are reflected in the following table,

	Teacher	Child
Role	to teach	to be moulded
Relationship	directive, arbitrary, powerful	powerless
Understanding	child as project, object, universal group	passive, a vessel waiting to be filled
Measure of Success	Outcomes driven	

It is that sense in which children are passive within this journey through education, which perhaps is the assumption that has the greatest undermining effect, and therefore must be addressed. The problem is that such thinking is not only pervasive but has come to be institutionalised, forming the very fabric of the system that we currently have.

JF: Having spent my professional life in schools I know how easy it is for practice to be influenced by those wider assumptions. However, it is important that we are continually prepared to challenge this.

> • What individuals or groups of children in your school have their experience of school shaped by adult assumptions? What are the implications of this?
>
> • Which parts of your current policy reflects assumptions that limit opportunities for partnership with children?
>
> • How does the way in which school is 'done' in the wider spaces (such as the playground or dining room) that makes up your school, reflect assumptions?

Constructing the 'schooled child'

Why is it that everything in our schools is so defined by age? What children are taught and when, what they eat, when they play, whom they share a classroom with and so on. There is an answer to this question, but it is probably not the one you might expect. The answer is 'age' is a useful tool for control!

Maybe this is too provocative? Well not really. For if we look at age we can see how it is a fairly recent feature in schools and one that now continues to take on a particular institutionalised meaning and which sits very comfortably alongside an image of the passive child, there to be moulded. This desire for schooling to be packaged reflected that need to identify strategies to deal with the increased visibility of children in the 19th Century as more and more people came into the towns. School was increasingly seen as a useful focus for these children and with this boom in schooling, age became the vehicle by which education was 'done'. It is important to stress that this was new. Age had never had this significance before, as schools reflected that need for flexibility (as children continued to support their families through work) so that classes contained children that would be at a similar academic level but could be very different ages.

However, defining education for children by ages and the associated stages that grew up alongside it, still continues to be pervasive. It reflects work from theorists such as Thorndike and Skinner with their emphasis on teaching as a learned behaviour, which was so significant in shaping the focus of schools in the first part of the 20th Century. Such ideas also provide a backbone to other psychological models including the work of Jean Piaget, which arguably continues to play an even greater role in practices within school.

Piaget's work cannot simply be dismissed as having a negative impact on educational theory, as his ideas contributed so much to the field. But, one of the limiting factors of his work was the stress that was placed on age as a defining factor in children's ability to manage, process and respond to interactions. He talks of six stages of development;

> The first three take place within a child's first two years and are characterised through the recognition of reflex actions, developing into first motor habits and, later, sensorimoter activities. The fourth stage, between the ages of two and seven years, is linked to intuitive

behaviour characterised by egocentricity, although it is only between the ages of seven and twelve that the child begins to use logic in shaping both social and moral interaction. But it is not until the child is twelve that the capacity to think in abstract terms marks the move into the adult world. (Frankel, 2012: 16).

Despite those aspects of Piaget's work that offer a more child focused approach to our understandings of learning it is the focus on age that has become such a significant institutional skeleton in the classrooms 'closet'. It is one that leaves those adults in school constantly asking are children 'ready' to engage with taking on a particular topic, whether that be in relation to recognised subject areas or in relation to themes such as sex education. As a result, it moves the child no further on from the socially limited and universal child that is portrayed above. (Also note Talcott Parson's socialisation theory, which has had an impact on the passive way in which children are positioned in relation to school).

Some of you may be thinking 'what is all the fuss about'? These theories stem from recognised academics and who are we to question them? Indeed you would be right to challenge, but wrong to simply accept these views. The reason for this is that these theories are built on adult assumptions of childhood, expected understandings of children, rather than drawing off an understanding of the child themselves. It was an acknowledgement of children's social competence that was going to lead to a revolution in the way in which we are now free to think about and engage with children.

A new emphasis: the individual child

In reaction to the work of writers such as Piaget and Parsons, others were seeking to present a challenge to the restricted and partial views of children. Such work highlighted the weakness of an assumed understanding of the child, and sought to engage children in a social context that they recognised and were able to make sense of. For example, research looked to repeat Piaget's experiments in different contexts which were more relevant to children's everyday lives, and using techniques, such as puppets to engage the children in the questions they were being asked (Donaldson and McGarrigle, 1975 and Donaldson and Hughes, 1979). Through such work and the research that followed, it became clear that the social aspect of the child must be acknowledged and that our understanding of children must have reference to the social context of their lives. This was further reflected in Piaget's own discipline by the work of Vygotsky and his assessment of the importance of the social in our understanding of the child, showing that a developmental model may have some relevance, but only within a framework that recognises the reality of children's social lives and the active nature of their engagement with it.

It is important to note that such thinking was not restricted to academia but that attitudes towards children were beginning to shift internationally at the highest levels. Following the International Year of the Child at the end of the 1970's, it took a further decade for the countries of the world to agree a document that defined rights to all children. The United Nations Convention on the Rights of the Child was almost universally accepted, adding further to a statement in favour of recognising the value of the child. Although it is easy to challenge the extent to which children have actually been empowered through such rights (which notably were defined by adults), as adults continue to control access to them, the rights agenda does offer a significant statement about the need to value children and to recognise their potential as participants within society.

As the Convention was being signed, another important statement was being shaped. Since those early challenges to the work of Piaget and others, academics from a variety of disciplines had started to further their research into our understanding of the child, with a clear intention to move beyond the accepted assumptions of the past. From anthropology to psychology to sociology and beyond, writing emerged that increasingly recognised the complex and subtle ways in which children were taking part in the social world. In 1990, academics Allison James and Alan Prout (1997) brought together these different views, establishing a foundation for Childhood Studies, which at its heart recognised the active engagement of children in their social worlds. Key themes included recognising childhood as a social construct, defined and shaped according to time and place. As well as acknowledging the active

31

nature of children as participants in the social world around them. Children were no longer to be seen in terms of what they might 'become' but rather as a 'being' in the here and now. This contrast with the assumptions of the past are reflected in the table below,

Traditional	Progressive
Passive	Active (a social agent)
Universal	Individual
Socially Incompetent	Socially Competent
Becoming (future orientated)	Being (engaging with here and now)
Sponge	Meaning Maker

The implications this has for the way in which we now think about policy and practice for children should not be underestimated. It offers a new foundation to shape the way we engage with children, one in which the competence and the voice of the child is given a value which had previously been ignored. This can be seen simply in the way in which children are involved in research and the value that is attached to their participation, as children's own words open windows into a world that had previously not been acknowledged by adults.

As a result, research has grown to reflect the strategic way in which children can be seen to make sense of their social worlds. A defining example of this for Childhood Studies is reflected in the research box below.

Example from Research: children as meaning makers

One extraordinary piece of work that has set the standard for so much of what has followed was the work of Myra Bluebond-Langner (1978). Her research focused on children who were terminally ill and literally lifted the lid on the reality of children's experiences of managing and coping with their illnesses.

> Children are capable of choosing behaviour so as to affect the way others see them. Children who know they are dying but wish to conceal this knowledge from their parents can, by doing some of the things that normal children do, momentarily change their parents view.

> A form of behaviour common among terminally ill children, 'exhibition of wounds', underlines how children try to affect not only the way others see them but also how they see themselves. By showing where and how they have been poked and prodded, children present themselves to others as sick and find their self image confirmed. This is further evidenced by the fact that once children internalise this view of self, they no longer use this strategy, except when meeting someone for the first time and wanting, for a number of reasons, to affect the stranger's view of them...

> The children's interpretation of themselves, others, and objects and the consequent action taken varies with the social, physical and temporal settings. A child's failure to discuss his or her own prognosis in the presence of adults, compared to open discussions in the presence of other children is one illustration... (pages 9-10)

This is now one of many examples that shows children actively shaping and defining their social worlds at every level and in every space. It reflects the contrast between adult assumptions of the child characterised by passivity, and the reality of the active way in which children actually come to manage the social world around them. Rather than children simply being shaped by adults and society more widely, children are interacting, making their own meanings that come to influence what they think and how they act. In short, these ideas demand that our engagement with children should be based on a recognition of social competence, rather than incompetence defined by certain ages and stages. It is a stance that has a range of implications for the way we do school, as our approach to the child comes to be based on an alternative foundation.

Agency

Defining this alternative foundation for approaching the child, means engaging with one more theoretical term, that of 'agency'. Although agency is a broad area of investigation, here what is important is a realisation of what an understanding and willingness to use this term in relation to children in schools offers. For recognising the child as a social agent, allows us to re-position the child in school. It is that sense of agency that sits at the heart of our definition of the social learner that was introduced earlier.

Agency as a term recurs in a number of fields as it reflects the ability of the individual to shape, frame and construct meaning. It is on the basis of the theories above that it is possible to extend these notions of agency to children themselves. What childhood studies considers is the need for children to be seen as 'agents', actively creating and constructing meanings as a response to the interactions that make up their social lives. This capacity as an agent is not limited to children who have achieved a certain age, but research is increasingly arguing that agency can be assigned to the youngest of children as they make sense of the world around them.

Agency must be seen as developing within a framework. That framework is shaped by those structures of the institutions and culture that surround us as well as our own personal experiences and our never ending quest to define our own identities. That search for 'self' places us in the middle of a set of dynamic and continual processes within which we are always assessing ourselves in relation to others. This sees us framing meanings based on what others do or say, how they look and behave. It provides a basis for understanding themes such as self esteem, peer pressure and our desire to belong.

A by-product of agency is the ability of the individual to construct meanings. This is significant as it offers a very different understanding of children to that presented by theorists such as Piaget. Rather than children's social competence being defined by the moments when they reach a certain milestone marked by age, children's understanding of the social world becomes continual and ongoing and places the child actively at the centre of this process of knowledge formation as they grow in experience. Such an awareness presents significant responsibilities to adults, particularly in relation to engagement but it also offers incredible possibilities to improve outcomes for children, as adults rather than working *on* children, work *with* children to establish a relevant partnership that allows children to navigate the complex social world they are part of.

The implication for viewing children in terms of their agency is challenging and exciting for schools. It offers a tremendous opportunity that can alter, encourage and reinforce the learning process as it moves away from an environment in which adults and children are set apart, to a context in which they are partners on a shared journey, where both parties bring value of their own.

Example from Research: Sociology in Learning

This case study reflects on the work of Andrew Pollard author of the popular 'reflective teaching in schools' book and chair of the Teaching and Learning Research Project.

Andrew Pollard is one who has written in favour of a 'sociology for learning in primary school' (1994). Within this early work he stressed the need for adults to engage with children as individuals and how through engaging more with children's identity and how this comes to be expressed, adults can be in a better position to support children with their learning. However, it is by accepting children in terms of their agency that Pollard's work makes the most significant statement as he states the case for partnership within schools. He says

Teaching and other forms of support by adults are necessary, but they are not sufficient. Learning also requires conditions, which enable each child to control the assembly and construction of their understanding. (Pollard, 1994: 22)

Within this the adults' role changes from one in which they simply direct teaching to a role to which they are encouraged to act as a reflective agent 'providing meaningful and appropriate guidance and extension to the cognitive structuring and skill development arising from the child's initial experiences' (Pollard, 1994: 22). It points to a different formula for approaching children in schools, one in which their capacity as agents influences the nature of the relationship they have with their teachers and the way in which learning is consequently done. It offers a foundation for engagement in learning that is relevant and effective. In some senses he points to a theoretical loophole that had emerged (and continues to have an impact) in learning where the social dimension was not fully considered or valued. However, he argues that it is only by acknowledging the child as an individual shaping and creating meanings as part of their social interactions that learning can really be understood.

Only children themselves can 'make sense', understand, and learn (1994: 22)

This statement should not be underestimated for the importance that it brings to the classroom. For rather than continuing to pursue a model in which children are seen as passive and as a result defined by ages and stages of development, Pollard is recognising that learning is a product of individual agency, albeit one that exists within the limitations of certain defining structures. As such, school is a place where one can start to engage with the development of the individual's identity and their attitudes to future learning, as part of a learning career that Pollard hopes will extend beyond formal schooling.

In a more recent piece of writing as part of a large and expansive project called the Teaching and Learning Research Project, Pollard draws on these earlier ideas in a research briefing titled 'education, schooling and learning for life: how meaning and opportunity build from everyday relationships' (TLRP, 2007). In it he sets out five steps to creating the lifelong learner, recognising the context and the individual dimension on which any learning journey builds. In this document he refers to the extent to which the number of social 'things' we are managing increases as we get older, therefore the importance of creating a toolkit to equip children to deal with 'all' this must not be ignored. He says

> Our analysis stands in stark contrast to the narrow target setting of many contemporary, centrally directed, education systems. Such approaches tend to emphasise formal aspects of provision and to over simplify teaching and learning processes. Maximising the potential of children and young people calls for a more appropriate understanding of them as social actors within their cultures and communities, and of how education fits into, and contributes to, their lives as a whole. TLRP 2007

As such what Pollard and others have promoted is an approach to education within which one is concerned not just with attainment in its rawest sense, but attainment in the context of children's individual social identities. This means that a response to learning is fundamentally shaped by the way in which the individual thinks about themselves and others in the context of their wider everyday lives.

Conclusion

The constructed views of childhood shared at the beginning which presents the child in terms of passivity universality, social incompetence and an over reaching need for control are influencing children's experience of school today. A desire for children to break away from these assumptions and to establish a relationship in which their sense of agency is recognised is highlighted in this response to a national school competition which asked children to define the school they wished to attend. One child wrote that they wished for

> a respectful school where we are not treated as empty vessels to be filled with information, where teachers treat us as individuals, where children and adults talk freely to each other and our opinion matters. (Cited in James and James, 2004: 139)

It is only by re-establishing the foundation on which education is based that a move towards such a system can ever be obtained. Current legislative developments continue to suggest an approach that maintains a reliance on those traditional assumptions stated above. Change, therefore, lies in the hands of those who are involved in putting the system into practice. This means that if we are going to address ethos, we need to question our own attitudes towards children as we start a transformation that looks beyond assumptions about the child and focuses on the individual child themselves.

Creating Change - Ethos:

- Your school ethos: what is it and who knows it?
- What are the principles, values and beliefs that underpin your ethos?
- What assumptions do you need to challenge, what compromises are you willing to make?
- What do you consider, the teaching staff consider and non-teaching staff consider to be the place of children in your school?

Case Study Examples - Ethos

Two of our case study schools (Keen and Eager - School 3 and A Way Forward - School 5) started their journey by effectively presenting the school community with a blank sheet – on which to invite ideas on ethos. They used training days to explore their school ethos and the principles and beliefs that they felt should underpin their thinking and actions. For both schools this highlighted the fact that although both had 'mission statements, strap lines and/or key words' these meant very little to the staff and children within their schools. There had been no conscious effort or actions to translate these promising intentions as reflected in these mission statements into effective and meaningful practice.

However, having been involved in and grappling with the *social learning agenda*, both schools have made their values much more explicit; children, parents and staff have a greater knowledge and understanding of ethos. A common sense of purpose and consistent language has developed which has supported the development of both schools.

Another of our case study schools (Slow and Steady - School 4) did not start the journey at what we would perceive to be the beginning and although positive developments have taken place and children are benefitting as a result, many staff consider the developments a 'bolt on'. As a consequence, there has been no fundamental re-engagement with ethos, as such it has not had the impact that it could have had.

Note: these examples will be developed in more detail in later sections, as we think about that journey of change. A template that we have used to consider this and which is loosely followed in these reviews reflect:

- an assessment of the facts
- what key issues were involved
- detailing possible solutions
- an analysis of solutions (as decide what to do)
- steps for implementation

You might find this a useful model for reflecting on change in your own schools.

Building block 2 – *community*: design a space for the social learner

Introduction

	Social Learning Aim	Pillar Two: Community	Principles or Drivers
The Social Learner	Allowing the individual child to grow in their awareness of themselves and others. Equipping children with knowledge and skills so that they can successfully navigate the complexities of the social world they are part of. Providing a foundation to maximise the child's learning potential in school and to increase children's participation and engagement in their families and communities.	Community: design a space for the social learner	Actively embrace the opportunities for social learning through the different spaces within school (and beyond)
			Defined efforts to build 'communities' at different levels throughout school
			A commitment to nurturing and maintaining a sense of belonging (for children and staff)
			An accepted understanding of the different parts/roles all members of the school community play in furthering social learning
			A recognition of home as key site for social learning

It is all well and good us talking about the agency of the child, but you know as well as I, this will not bring about change, for one of the most influential drivers in school is the 'organisational culture', those 'institutional' processes that shape so much of what we do in school and how we do it. The organisational cultures that develop in schools reflect some of those themes picked up in the last chapter, such as keeping children in classes according to age, through to what people wear and what they are called (Mrs, Miss, Mr). However, it also impacts on what schools see as important, as testing criteria are set and staff find ways of meeting those targets, as best they can. In short it establishes a structure within which school comes to be done. A defining feature of the current culture within schools is the value placed on children being 'taught to be' (reaching a set of predefined, academically driven criteria), as opposed to children having the opportunity to 'learn to do' (being engaged in the process of their own learning). The problem is that the existing structure is easy to pass on, but it is not as easy to break.

Here is an example. We all could probably agree that a great way to develop a sense of community within a classroom is by having the children and their teacher come up with a classroom code, a constitution if you like. The only problem is that the effectiveness of such an idea will be shaped by the existing culture in the school. Is that school community a place where children are 'taught to be' or a space within which children 'learn to do'?

One piece of research reflected on this process of establishing a classroom code. It looked at the attitude that teachers brought to this, as they sought to create a community within their classroom at the beginning of the school year. Despite inviting the children's input, the process was undermined by the strength of the culture that pervaded the school, which meant that teachers approached this process thinking that:

1. the teacher knows best
2. children cannot participate constructively in the development of a classroom constitution

3. children want and expect the teacher to determine the rules of the game

4. children are not interested in the constitution

5. children should be governed by what a teacher thinks is right and wrong, but a teacher should not be governed by what children think is right or wrong.

6. the ethics of adults are obviously different from and superior to the ethics of children

7. children should not be given responsibility for something they cannot handle or for which they are not accountable

8. if constitutional issues were handled differently, chaos might result

(Sarason, 1971: 176)

The teachers in this study were horrified when they heard the results as it was not their intention to approach the children and their collective efforts to create a community in this way. The point is that, despite this example being dated, the culture of schooling continues to be such that it predisposes us towards seeing children as being 'taught to be' rather than recognising those processes of 'learning to do'. If we are going to allow the social learner to thrive, then we need to take on this notion of community and to recognise and react to some of the pervading themes that have so limited school as a space, in order to acknowledge the social dimensions to learning. The difference between a culture focused on 'taught to be' rather than 'learn to do' is laid out in the table below.

	Taught to be		Learn to do
Learning (defined by)	Performance		Process
Children (seen as)	Universal Group	vs	Individuals
Structure	Rigid		Co-constructed

JF: One of the significant challenges I faced when I arrived at Time to Change - School 2, was that a culture had developed that did not value learning. The school was a failing school by every measure. It was a school which, like many others, had lost touch with the value of learning. The problem was that no-one thought the right idea might be to try and change an ongoing desire to impose a model that was focused on the children being 'taught to be', as they were moulded to reach the standards that the system had set them. What this school needed was a community that did not focus on performance but on the process of learning, that had room to respond to children as individuals. In short it needed to ignite a passion for learning, that if done right would also mean that those performance targets were not impossible.

The current system in so many of our schools is focused on results. We are asking where children will be when they leave our schools before they even arrive. We want to place children into those boxes that match a given criteria of what 'success' is meant to be. We know where they should go on our graphs and spreadsheets and we are also aware of the consequences if we do not succeed. Children are therefore seen as a universal group, who will be judged on their ability to attain and achieve predefined targets. It is an approach that does not give enough weight to the 'processes' involved in learning. Learning as a journey, as a voyage of discovery in which the individual will get the chance to widen their knowledge of the world by drawing from and taking interest in a great many things, but also with the time and space to further their own personal lines of enquiry, to think about what they find interesting. In a 'learn to do' approach, it is the individual who is placed at the centre and it is the individual that is the focus of a culture in which they become equipped with the skills to develop knowledge, rather than simply given a predefined catalogue of what they should know.

The relevance of schools

It is not surprising that the structures of our schools, the way we do things, are hard to break when we realise that they are very deeply rooted in the history of schooling. Chris Watkins (2005) notes that ever since the earliest schools, 5000 years ago, the approach, which for many he suggests, still continues today, has been 'learning = being taught' (2005: 48). Such an approach sits very comfortably alongside those constructions of childhood, considered in the last chapter, in which the child was understood as a vessel waiting to be filled, as a sponge, passive and universal, dependent on 'teachers' (in the widest sense) for a bank of knowledge that they were given. Such an approach, as was suggested, limits an expectation of the child: 'too often we believe schools underestimate children and young people and focus on what children cannot do rather than what they can' (Wringley et al, 2012: 2). The result is not just a reassertion of past constructions of childhood and the de-valuing of the child but it also calls into question the relevance of schools themselves.

As a result of the past, schools today are, for too many, simply a production line.

Society shapes that production line. At one end, as early as possible the child or 'product' is put onto the line. Then, the product begins to be shaped, placed into pre-prepared moulds designed by adults. If the product is not able to assume the shape required, it is taken off the production line. 'Knowledge', in this analogy is a quantifiable liquid devised by adults, which is continually dropped into the product. At a number of points the product receives testing. This looks solely at the amount of 'knowledge' that the 'product' is able to retain. As a result of this testing a selection is made to release a lower grade product into stores with no further testing or to allow the product to continue on the line in order to receive further 'knowledge' and testing and an additional stamp of 'quality'. At no point is the product tested for anything other than the amount of 'knowledge' it retains.

Do we want our schools to simply be there, as Carol Dweck (2006) so significantly asks, to point out to children what they 'can do' and what they 'don't know' rather than equipping them to recognise their potential and to explore and discover with skills that allow them to take on what they 'can't do' and what they 'want to know'? Surely schools should be about providing children with 'knowledge' in its broadest sense, supporting the child as a resourceful and engaged 'learner', impacting not just their future, but importantly their present too.

As Wringley et al (2012) make clear, 'schools must change because they do not help produce human beings with the resources to live fruitful lives' (Wringley et al 2012: 196). This position is grounded on their belief that the role of school should be to help 'young people to become fully human, individually and collectively'(195). They are not alone in arguing that schools must change to recognise this aspect of their role.

> Their [schools] ultimate goal must be to enhance pupils progress, achievement and development in the broadest sense, to capture the breadth of what it is likely to take to flourish in the twentieth century. (Stoll and Bolam, 2005: 54)

It offers a vision for schooling that suggests that schools should be concerned with both those traditional requirements for attainment and the need for children to build and develop a bank of knowledge that allows them to skilfully engage with and manage the world around them. Success, therefore, is not just about academic levels but also about the ability of the child to effectively navigate their way through the world around them. Children are social learners.

The value of learning

Re-defining a community that embraces the 'social leaner' means schools being prepared to take on these cultural assumptions about how schooling should be done. It is rather frightening that at a time when research is increasingly recognising the need for change, school policy continues to be battening down the hatches and finding ways to defend their traditions.

Academic Chris Watkins (2008), talks of how policy approaches have led to a depoliticisation, a demoralisation and a depersonalization in schools. Depoliticisation reflects the pressures on the teacher to conform to given criteria (currently this could be seen in terms of performance related pay). Demoralisation is the extent to which schools are restricted in encouraging a moral dimension, as a focus on what works and what customers want prevails over what is best. Finally, and perhaps most worryingly, he draws out the extent to which depersonalisation reflects a system that is simply not set up to value the individual as 'one size fits all' (2008: 7). Under these conditions the range of identities available to pupils is severely limited such that children themselves are concerned about their value should they not fit the criteria that adults have established. As one 11 year old said in relation to taking standardised tests, 'So I'm frightened I'll do the SATS and I'll be a nothing' (Watkins, 2008: 7).

Such an agenda has created a tension around the value of simply learning and about our ambitions for the individual. In primary schools one might argue that the value lies in teaching that produces results, creating the effective reader and mathematician, rather than in enabling the learner. What is so disappointing is that this is sitting in increasing contrast to both academic and popular views.

A popular view:

New York Times columnist David Brooks in his internationally best selling book *The Social Animal* sets out to re-define what our focus, not just in schools, but for life should be. It is a direct challenge to the US educational system that he argues, as a result of misplaced priorities, is not serving children or society as well as it could. Right at the beginning, he outlines the characters that he shapes the book around. Brooks highlights how these creations are not the most intelligent, not the most beautiful, not the best at sport, but they were successful. They were successful because:

> They were energetic, honest and dependable. They were persistent after setbacks and acknowledged their mistakes. They possessed enough confidence to take risks and enough integrity to live up to their commitments… they knew how to read people, situations and ideas. The skills the master seamen has to navigate the oceans they had to navigate the world. (2012: xiff)

An academic view:

The value of social skills is not offered here as provocative fiction but as views based on increasing amounts of data. Indeed research in education both in Europe (Dahlberg, 2011) and the United States (Spodek and Saracho, 2013) is highlighting not just the importance of social skills to the individual but the value of those skills to learning itself. 'Increasingly researchers are confirming a link between school success and young children's emotional knowledge' (Denham, Zinsser, Brown, 2013: 73), as they encourage a move from 'literacy and numeracy' to recognising the 'whole child'. This is necessary as it is the 'socially successful child [who] is in a position to thrive' (Denham, Zinsser, Brown, 2013:67).

This need to recognise the social dimension of children's learning as a fundamental part of a desire to further attainment is reflected in other reports such as the Teacher and Learning Research Programme (2007), the findings of the Cambridge Review (2010) and even government sponsored inquiries such as the Education Endowment Funds investigation (Gutman and Schoon, 2013) of non cognitive skills.

An important undercurrent in many of these analyses is how shifting the balance of our focus towards the learner carries with it the power for bringing about real change.

> Learning refers not just to the transmission of knowledge but also to change in emotions, sensations and feelings as well as being tied into wider collective forces of transformation (Jarvis and Parker, 2005)' (McCulloch and Woodin, 2010: 136).

At a time of crisis in education in many western countries the opportunity for transformation is an exciting proposition. The problem is transformation means 'transformation' and that includes re-evaluating the way in which we see school as a space, as we look to create a community of learning that allows the individual child to thrive.

JF: A message from the heart. Transformation is a challenge but a challenge that is worth the time, effort, frustrations and the personal commitment involved since the result has a significant

impact on the children as learners. Too often we spend enormous amounts of time tweaking the system, making it fit, reacting to the next initiative and in most cases to limited impact. It is time to stand back and consider, in the broadest terms, the purpose of education in and for the 21st Century, take control and redirect our attention and focus onto something that is more 'worthwhile' and of great value.

Positioning the social learner

Drawing off the definition of the child as a social agent from the last chapter, the result is that children 'are not passive recipients but active constructors of classroom communities' (Etheridge, 2004: 101). It is, therefore, only by establishing the right atmosphere, within which the social dimension of a child's learning is accepted that the *social learning agenda* can progress (it is a model that in some senses is reflected in approaches such as Montessori education). It means having a clear ambition for the 'culture' of our school, one which returns us to the question of relevance. Is school simply to see that children pass tests, or should it be about something so much more? As Carol Dweck challenges us, 'is success about learning or proving you're smart?' (2006: 16) She demands that we really think about our attitude to education and the extent to which we are opening a door of limitless possibilities or simply setting a fixed and defined barrier of achievement that some will reach and others will not. If learning is simply teaching, as it is for so many (see above), then it is about judging 'permanent traits' rather than saying to the child, 'you are a developing person and I am interested in your development' (2006: 172).

This idea of managing potential is so important for as Hargreaves (2004) highlights if schools get it right then they can create a platform for learning that does not end at the same time as an individual's school career but that goes on forever. In doing so, primary schools are instrumental in shaping lifelong learning and have the potential to promote an ambition in the individual to manage the 'projects' that they face in their lives, drawing off a bank of skills and abilities as they seek to 'learn' their way through.

The following 'example from research' offers a sense of how a school can embrace the active way in which children are engaged with their learning. It is an 'ambition' that has significant implications for how both the child and their teachers come to be positioned. What stands out, is the extent to which the space within school, becomes a shared space for furthering a joint ambition to learn. It is that focus on the process of learning, that becomes essential in a *social learning agenda*.

Examples from Research: A learning community - Chris Watkins (2005)

The challenge for schools, therefore, is to create a community that allows for and values the 'learner'. Any old 'community' in school will not do, it 'depends on the values which develop, and the best is achieved through a caring, pro-social, learning orientated approach to the relations between all parties' (Watkins 2005: 50). Watkins moves us on from ethos and demands that we think about that arena for learning that comes to be created.

Watkins argues that through creating a sense of community, children feel as though they belong and this has implications in relation to attainment. With reference to a large study in secondary schools he shows how the results 'revealed that students' gains in achievement and engagement were significantly higher in schools with practices derived from thinking of the school as a community' (p49). Such results are reflected in work in primary schools too.

This sense of community drives motivation as children feel as though they belong within a set of relationships based on trust. (It highlighting yet again how we must be conscious of a social dimension to children's learning. By recognising children as engaged in their social worlds, we can understand not only why belonging could be seen as important but also we can explain how this helps with learning and what steps can be taken to improve this where it is lacking). Notably Watkins suggests that having established that sense of belonging there is a higher likelihood that children will participate.

Helpfully Watkins offers some examples for what these communities might look like. The first reflects the basic requirements, progressing to the third which presents the fully integrated learning community.

Each level of community raises the centrality of partnership to the process of the individual's learning.

1. Classroom as communities
2. Classrooms as communities of learning
3. Classrooms as learning communities

Under the first category Watkins reflects on how a sense of community creates:

- students that are more engaged
- increased sense of belonging, leading to greater participation and motivation
- shared responsibility
- difference is not a problem and diversity is embraced

This is not the aim though. Having established that sense of community the teacher can then seek to further this in the second category where learning becomes an integral part of the community itself, with the following results:

- increased engagement in leading and high level engagement in the discipline
- learning from and helping each other
- motivated to learn for its own sake, to make choices and feel responsible for what happens to them
- enhanced individual outcomes on important aspects of individual learning

This is not the aim though! Watkins continues to reflect on the extent to which learning remains driven by adults. He wants a learning community in which this partnership between the child and adult is jointly driven.

'a learning community operates on the understanding that the growth of knowledge involves individual and social processes. It aims to enhance individual learning that is both a contribution to their own learning and the groups learning, and does this through supporting individual contributions to a communal effort' (p57)

Such a 'community' builds on the ideas that are the focus for this book, as an effective learning community can only exist by children demonstrating high levels of social skills in engaging with and working alongside both their peers and the adults. The result,

- disciplined discourse becomes part of the community
- responsibility for and control of knowledge becomes shared.
- conceptions of learning are richer and co-constructive
- shared metacognition develops about the process of learning

Wouldn't it be so exciting to have a classroom that operated like this? The point is that it is not impossible. Through recognising the social capacity of the child, their role as a social learner, and then by creating the culture within a community in which they are free to thrive, an independent learner can emerge. This is not an approach that is restricted to any particular level of the school system, but rather one that we should be aiming for, throughout.

A community of belonging

JF: I have worked in many schools and each school has a different sense of community. Having a community that is specific to your school must be right, however, what is important is that that community has space for the social leaner. I have been very encouraged by the fact that educationalists are increasingly talking about this difference between school as 'traditional' or 'progressive', and within the latter there is greater space for the individual child. But what progressive ends up looking like will be very different between schools.

It is an area that must also not simply be looked at from an adult perspective. It is never good enough to take for granted our perception of school as a community. The following is an extract from a piece of research we did into one of the challenges we were facing in school. The research itself, perhaps can be seen as simply reinforcing what we might have known, however the point is that we asked. It is in the asking and perhaps more so in the listening that as adults we can start to work with children to create a learning community that is shared.

Case Study - Time for Change - School 2 - Mobility and Belonging

Introduction
This investigation rose out of a concern about the impact of high mobility within the school. It follows on from a number of in school assessments of the situation. One of the themes that emerged from these was the possible effect that 'new' children might have on existing children and the dynamics within the classroom. The aim of this piece of research therefore, was to consider the perspective of children on 'new' children joining their class.

Methods
We initially planned a questionnaire as a means of starting to get some sense of the children's feelings on these issues, from which focus groups and interviews could follow.

A questionnaire was designed to look at a number of elements around this issue, dealing with:

1. Personal Information – hobbies, what they enjoyed learning, what they found challenging.

2. Do you belong? – at home, in the classroom, at school, with friends.

3. Feelings – responses to examples such as falling out with friends, starting a new school year, having a new teacher, changing learning tables and having a new child in the classroom.

4. Scenarios – considered children's impressions of the impact of having

   a. a new child introduced to the class,

   b. a 'new' child joining their table,

   c. a 'new' child asking to play with them in the playground and

   d. a 'new' child asking to sit with them at lunch.

   Note: Children were given a definition of belonging 'feeling like you fit in'.

The research was shared with 6 classes in key stage 2. 155 children took part (80 boys and 75 girls).

Headline Findings
The findings here are based on an initial analysis of mainly the quantitative data. These findings have been considered with respect to frequency, age, school class and gender.

Belonging:
The findings from the questionnaire did not seem to suggest that the children had particular concerns over new children entering their class. In fact many saw it as a positive. When asked how they felt when a new child was introduced to their class 91 of the children responded they felt good, with another 53 saying they felt okay. This positive response was reflected in all of the scenarios (although, to slightly different degrees, for example the children were slightly more cautious about a new child sitting on their learning table).

The children's sense of belonging was challenged most by starting a new school year, as well as having a new teacher, but this was nothing compared to the impact that falling out with friends had, with 115 children responding that it made them feel as though they fitted in a bit or a lot less.

The children responded that 'home' was the place that they felt they were least likely to belong with 50 children questioning or denying that they belonged. In the school and classroom children also had some doubt about their belonging. In 4 classes this amounted to ¼ of the children questioning their belonging.

There was a slight suggestion that as the children got older their ability to manage their sense of belonging and therefore cope with change, improved. For example on asking how the children felt about a new child entering the classroom the younger children focused more on the negatives, recording their feelings as not so good or really bad, whereas by age 10 and 11 years the children did not use these negative terms at all.

Concerns:

<u>Friendships</u>

As reflected above, an overriding theme in the children's concerns over 'new' children was the impact that it might have on their friendships. The children expressed worries over how they would manage existing friendships. For some this was positive,

> *I don't think it will effect anything it won't effect my friendship group they could even join in if they like.*

Many children seemed keen on the opportunity of welcoming a new child and taking on the role of guide and friend. For some it was more of a challenge,

> *it will effect my friendship because my friends might start to like him/her more than me.*

The fear over how a 'new' child might impact on an existing friendship group was a real concern, with potential to impact on children's learning and feelings at school.

<u>Learning</u>

The children were also aware about the impact a 'new' child might have on their learning.

> *somebody new is on my table but I can still focus*

As this child suggests, it will change the dimensions and within this they will need to find a way to respond, here the child suggests they will still be able to 'focus'. As this example suggests this concern was most clearly seen in the scenario about having someone new joining their table. Although the response was generally positive, children expressed concerns over whether the 'new' child would distract them from their learning. This was indicated by concerns that the 'new' child might 'chat a lot'. In relation to actual learning the children also noted that because they were new

> *he/she might don't know about the subjects and he she will ask questions*

It was a fear that 'sometimes it [a new person] distracts your learning' that the children were concerned about.

Conclusion

The questionnaire holds some really interesting data that the school can make use of. From this initial review of the data, themes have emerged that should encourage recognition of

- The generally positive response to welcoming 'new' children and the desire of existing children to support and integrate them.
- The theme of belonging both at home and in the classroom and the extent to which for some this is a challenge.
- The impact that friendship 'issues' have on children and their learning as well as their broader experience of school.
- A dedication (indeed a passion) to learning amongst the children.

There are lots of ways in which belonging can be encouraged within a learning community. We have seen children and teachers come together to ask important questions that have allowed engagement with this key theme of belonging. Questions that teacher have asked have included getting the children's views on,

- What is learning?
- How can we learn?
- How can we support others to learn?
- Who can we learn with?
- What ways can we manage challenges to our learning?

Once views have been shared these have then been displayed within the classroom. Notably these questions differ somewhat from a traditional classroom contract, for here those behavioural elements become implied in the focus on 'social learning'.

One of the questions that came out of the mobility project (see above) was the frequency that a classroom, as a learning community, should re-consider or re-state formally that sense of belonging. Of course the start of a school year is a good time for this. But, that does not mean it should be the only time. Dynamics within classrooms can change, particularly if new children are moving in (or out) and therefore that sense of belonging needs to be given space to evolve.

Other examples of engaging with belonging that we have seen include early years projects, which combine a desire to establish belonging with efforts to create a shared language for social engagement (see 'Speak' chapter later), or indeed school wide projects that draw off elements of the school ethos, for example, and link these to a series of assemblies supported by class based projects that are then brought together at a school level. For example, Keen and Eager - School 3 did a project around the Yellow Brick Road (from the Wizard of Oz), which brought the whole school together to look at aspects of the school as a learning community.

Belonging projects are not alien to school environments. What is important as part of the *social learning agenda* is the extent to which we understand that belonging is dynamic and therefore changing. Belonging is not simply a focus for the start of the school year, but for the whole of it. It is not something that can be imposed by adults but rather is the product of the individuals that make up a learning community. Lacking a sense of belonging can have significant implications for the individual learner, it is therefore a key ingredient for an effective school.

Parents

A learning community must also include parents. They can often be the final frontier.

Parents are involved in schools in a range of ways. Pollard (2014) sums this up in relation to three types of relationship.

- Parents as consumers - using school to provide an education but maintaining their distance

- Parents as resources - happy to provide help within school

- Parents as partners - engaged in supporting the children's learning

Notably these examples are focused around parents undertaking a role or engaging with their children's learning within school. An ambition of the *social learning agenda* is to look at the extent to which 'social learning' can become a focus that is not just about what happens within the confines of the school building but which spreads to those other arenas within which children live their lives including the home and their neighbourhoods.

Reports reflect the extent to which the family is significant in children's educational journey. One stark piece of research from the University of Bristol (Leckie et al, 2010) reflected that the home (at 40%) was the most significant factor in influencing variations in children's educational progress (alongside the child themselves (38%), the primary school (9%), secondary school (10%), the neighbourhood (2%) and the Local Education Authority (1%).

Understanding that relationship and engaging with the issues that it raises are therefore important features of developing an effective learning community. For us it marks a significant area for further consideration.

Case Study - Time for Change School 2 - Parenting

The contrast between Parent Power - School 1 and Time for Change - School 2 could not have been more stark. At Parent Power - School 1 parental opinions were never hard to find. Parents wanted to be in every aspect of their children's schooling, which was often supported with a view on how that aspect of their child's schooling should be conducted. Time for Change - School 2, on the other hand was a place that parents felt they were under an obligation to take their child to. The school represented authority, as a consequence for many, any engagement with those who represented that authority was to be avoided. As such, parents starting point with school was a lack of trust, which is not a strong foundation to seek their engagement in building a learning community.

This did not stop parents being invited to get involved from opportunities to read with their children in early years, to come and be part of collaborative learning days in key stage 2. However, it was not until the third year of John's time at School 2 that a focus on parent's place as part of the learning community became really visible. This was made possible by employing a family worker. The role of the family worker, which evolved over time, was effectively to act as a point of contact between staff, children and their parents. It directly addressed those issues of trust that had for too long been a barrier, through a position that allowed time to be given to building relationships.

This saw a journey from informal conversations, to coffee mornings through to a focused parenting programme. Indeed, it was a significant achievement to see parents regularly attending a programme that not only allowed them to reflect on their own practices, but also to consider how this supported their child as a learner.

Case Study - Keen and Eager School 3 - Engaging Parenting

If children's learning potential is ever going to be fully harnessed, then those at home need to be involved. Engaging families in the *social learning agenda* takes time, however Keen and Eager - School 3 as part of searching for ways to bridge the gap between the classroom and the sitting room, have started sending home information sheets, in the form of a newsletter that allows parents to engage directly with the practices being developed in school, in a format that staff and children already understand.

These efforts mark how the school is recognising the role of parents in relation to building ethos, community, lead, speak and act, as they are being invited to participate in this learning community.

Conclusion

Establishing learning communities places a different value on school, not just from the outside but from the inside too. In a learning community the individual becomes central to their own learning - they are the key. It is no wonder that this leads to a greater sense of motivation and responsibility. What is so attractive is the extent to which it allows the learner to take control, to have some ownership which is the time when our engagement takes on a new dimension, when we truly start to learn. If you want to learn then you will!

Gatto shares an example of this. Before the 1850's there was no compulsory schooling in the State of Massachusetts. Once it did become compulsory children had to be rounded up by soldiers and taken to school, such was local dismay. At the time the literacy rate was 98%. However, ever since children were forced to go to school, until today the rate has never been higher than 91% (Gatto, 2005: 22) (his figures were based on research in the 1990's). Gatto also refers to home schooling where children's 'ability to think' is five or even ten years ahead of their formally trained peers' (Gatto, 2005: 22). The point is that it makes a difference if you have some sense of control over your learning. Is home the only place this can happen? No, schools can do it too, but it means a change of attitude, a change of culture and a restructuring of communities that places the social learner at the heart.

Creating Change - Community:

- What does the *social learning agenda* look like to you?
- What opportunities are there in your school to support social learning?
- How can you get pupils, staff and parents more involved in the *social learning agenda*?

Building block 3 – *lead*: championing a learning process

Introduction

	Social Learning Aim	Pillar Three: Lead	Principles or Drivers
The Social Learner	Allowing the individual child to grow in their awareness of themselves and others. Equipping children with knowledge and skills so that they can successfully navigate the complexities of the social world they are part of. Providing a foundation to maximise the child's learning potential in school and to increase children's participation and engagement in their families and communities.	Lead: championing a learning process	Defined, structured and driven vision for social learning.
			Commitment to professional development in furthering social learning at all levels.
			Effective channels of communication (through which to further vision, strengthen relationships, promote professional culture)
			Leadership embraced and encouraged at all levels (including with children) creating a culture to inspire.
			Ongoing recognition of the value of research for developing understandings of the child and of learning.

Are you a leader or a follower? I was at a conference where the then head of the British army was talking about leadership. Leadership is important but it is no good, he said, if the leader runs from their lines and approaches the objective only to look around and find out that no-one else has arrived there with them. It is the same in a school. You might have the most tremendous idea, but it is no good moving forward unless others wish to follow.

It is the role of the leader, at whatever level, to establish an environment that allows others to be partners in that change. Leadership is, therefore, about developing relationships of trust within which ideas can be shared, risks taken, debates had, evidence gathered and positive outcomes celebrated. Leadership is not about power, but about empowerment, and it is driven by effective communication within the context of relationships in which each person is respected and has a sense of the value of their role. Leadership should never remain the limited prerogative of a chosen few, but should reflect a way of approaching a school community, in which all are encouraged to lead.

Good leadership creates a context for effective transformation and change and is therefore an essential element for implementing a successful *social learning agenda.*

Brighouse and Woods (1999) describe a head teacher's career as having three phases. They suggest that during the first phase, 'initiation', the new head is wrestling with the unfamiliarity of being in this new position. During the 'development' phase the head teacher is established, has built up strong relationships and is able to drive forward initiatives for school improvement. 'Decline and withdrawal', is described as a brief evening when they lose their power and cease to plan for tomorrow. Pointedly, they go on to say that this 'evening' is for some not so brief!

This analysis is not restricted to head teachers. The challenge of feeling empowered and motivated to be part of change is real for a newly qualified teacher in the same way as it is for a member of a senior leadership team. Notably, a similar analogy can be created for children. The child enters school feeling uncertain, they then grow in confidence and start to engage, but as that engagement comes to be limited by the nature of the institution, so the child develops a sense of apathy, until each day is just going through the motions. The idea of a 'coasting school' can be so easily defined as a place where the learning community has forgotten what it means to innovate, such that each day is pretty much the same as the one before. It is a school that is on the path to 'decline and withdrawal'.

Why such an aggressive tone towards what might be good schools, doing a good job? The reason is simple, maintaining the status quo in education is not good enough. As internationally acclaimed educationalists such as Sir Ken Robinson (2006 Ted Talk) have said, it is no good that we are part of a process of 'evolution' within our schools because what is needed is a 'revolution'. Many have reflected on the opportunities that schools are presented with when a new head teacher comes into post (Coles and Southworth, 2005) but leading a revolution is not simply the job of those that have the title of 'head teacher', rather it is a mantle that all of us, whatever our roles in schools, must take on.

A foundation for change

Leading change, and specifically embracing a *social learning agenda*, involves creating the right temperature for transformation. As Stoll and Bolam (2005) suggest, it involves,

- Creating a culture for learning
- Ensuring learning for pupils and adults alike
- Attending to the human side of change
- Ensuring enquiry based practice
- Making connections
- Creating external conditions in which professional learning communities can thrive

Here however, we are just going to focus on the following,

1. Leading through Vision - 'Have an Idea'
2. Leading through Dialogue - 'Talk and Listen'
3. Leading through Personal Development - 'Keep on Learning'

One of the reasons that we have chosen these headings is that the call that is needed in schools is not one that is defined by the length of time that a head teacher spends in a school - what we are calling for is a lasting change. This demands that we in schools are thinking about our vision for education, that we are talking about it and that we are interested in learning more. At present, in reality it is likely that these elements will form part of a process of change, but what needs to be encouraged is a more ready climate within which change can happen.

By debunking the managerial speak, such that these ideas relate to having an idea, talking and listening and keeping on learning, we want schools to realise that this is something that we can all be involved in. So do not wait for a new head teacher, make your school one of vision, dialogue and learning and see what happens.

1. Leading through vision - 'have an idea':

JF: I am not sure when my focus moved from teaching to learning. Or when I realised that getting children 'ready to learn' through providing them with curricular opportunities that developed their everyday social skills was so vital to them becoming effective learners. I am not sure when I understood the importance of the link between providing children with strategies to resolve those social issues and the impact that had on their learning in the classroom. All I can say is that I am very pleased that I did and I only wish that I had developed these views as a focus earlier in my teaching career. This shift in thinking has come to dominate my work as a senior leader. This desire to position the child, in the context of their social world, at the centre of this process of learning has given me a 'vision' that has come to underpin my thinking in relation to school.

However, it is no good having a vision if one does not do something about it.

There is no doubt that many schools have a focus on developing children as 'life long learners' and senior leaders do speak about the importance of the 'individual child' and a 'holistic approach' but how many schools explicitly translate these intentions into planned and meaningful experiences across the whole school; embedding a 'vision' into day to day school practice.

Leadership through vision is therefore not only about having an idea, but about having the motivation to bring that idea to life, to make it visible, explicit and practical.

Making Social Learning Visible: Within a social learning context, the need for visibility is even more pronounced. Education has been 'done' in a particular way for a very long time, establishing firmly the role of the adult as teacher and the child as passive learner (as discussed earlier). Eliciting those process that are part of learning however demands a reconsideration of these roles, as John Hattie in his influential work Visible Learning (in which, through a statistical analysis he shows a link between success and the extent to which the process of 'learning' has been made visible) argues,

> 'what is most important is that teaching is visible to the student, and that the learning is visible to the teacher. The more the student becomes the teacher and the more the teacher becomes the learner, then the more successful are the outcomes (Hattie: 2009: 25 - see also 2012: 17).

For us, a focus on 'visible learning' can only happen when one is aware of what the social dimension of learning is. As such the *social learning agenda* has developed to support a change in roles, as well as to reflect an increased visibility to those previously hidden aspects of classroom engagement.

The hesitancy that some have around the 'social' dimension, increases the need to make it visible, both in terms of explanation and as proof of its value. It is no good having a vision, if one is not able to define it and to offer some practical application. In relation to promoting learning more generally, Chris Watkins (2009) talks of the need for schools to,

- Make learning an object of attention

- Make learning an object of conversation

- Make learning an object of reflection

To which John always adds,

- To make learning the focus of action for all.

To reinforce a vision for a *social learning agenda* we would subtly change this:

- Make social learning an object of attention

- Make social learning an object of conversation

- Make social learning an object of reflection

- To make social learning the focus of action for all

It is through making social learning visible and practical that it becomes a real part of change and not a passing theory that one acknowledges but struggles to define and finds even harder to associate with progress. Naturally the visibility of a vision will increase as that vision begins to establish itself in the practices of a school, but those efforts to make your vision explicit are most effective when pursued right from the beginning.

The *social learning agenda* provides a vision, an 'idea'. It is a vision that does not work if it simply remains in the mind's eye of one person, even of two or three. Rather it is a vision that needs to be shared and more than that, needs to take on a form and to become part of practice. Leadership is key to acknowledging that vision (whether direct from a head teacher or others), to being motivated to pursue it and in making it visible such that it can become a project that is the focus of all within a learning community.

Case Study - Time for Change - School 2 - John's experience of putting an idea into practice

JF: After having accepted the role as head teacher, I had a vision and although at the time it was not defined by the heading *social learning agenda* (as we hadn't invented that yet), it carried a desire to make the school a place

> 'in which the teachers...and its administrators continuously seek and share learning, and act on their learning. The goal of their actions is to enhance their effectiveness as professionals for the 'students' benefits; thus this arrangement may also be termed communities of continuous inquiry and improvement'. (Astuto, Clark, Read, McGree and Fernandez, 1993)

To make it so, I knew I needed to immediately draw out the role of the individual child within this process of learning and to make what they were experiencing the focus for inquiry and improvement. Due to the nature and context of the school it was important for me to move fast. As a result I needed some quick 'wins' as I sought to promote the child as an active learner and so I introduced the school to the notion of the 6 'R's drawn from work by Guy Claxton (2002) and Bill Lucas (2005) (this work is looked at more in the next chapter). In drawing from both we ended up with the following R's:

Responsibility
Resilience
Resourcefulness
Reasoning
Reflection
Respect

I had used a version of this strategy in 'Parent Power' - School 1 and in other schools, however, in those instances I had the leisure of being able to work the vision through the schools so that it evolved as a community project. In this situation 'swifter action was required'. Each of our agreed Rs (there were six) were introduced through assemblies on a Monday, giving me the chance to talk to the children (and importantly the staff too!) about the R's and how they might help us to shape our learning community. (Indeed, I changed the school motto from simply a 'spirit to succeed', which was important to these children, to 'a learning community with a spirit to succeed'). The assemblies could then be followed up in class on a Tuesday, as I included little discussion starters in the registers. These could then fit in informally to situations that came up in lessons, as well as providing more formal opportunities within PSHE and circle time. Each week we would also finish on Friday with a celebration assembly that allowed us to highlight through real life examples some of what the children had done that week and how these actions reflected the week's theme. At the same time weekly newsletters were written to parents focussing on the different aspects of learning the children were exploring.

This desire to make social learning visible, was not just for the sake of the children but also and perhaps more challengingly for the staff. Sometimes, when there is a culture in which vision is overt and in which dialogue and personal development are real, change can be readily received. Here, the change needed to be quick and I had not had a chance to develop strong relationships with the staff as a whole, so for some this focus on the child as an active learner took them outside of their comfort zone. Although, for many there was a realisation that change was needed, that the children had not been served well and that as a result they were willing to give almost anything a try. It meant that staff meetings became devoted to exploring the characteristics of each of the 6Rs in terms of:

- making them 'visible and explicit',
- planning curricular opportunities through which the children could experience and develop the 6Rs,
- considering the behaviours that the children might exhibit when demonstrating any of the 6Rs.

It was vital that teachers 'knew and understood' what lay behind the vision and that this had practical meaning to them. We explored this through themes such as:

- The need for shared values and vision
- Collective responsibility throughout school
- Reflective professional (and child based) inquiry
- Promoting collaborative and group learning

As a result the teachers could then start to consider those links between a focus on the social dimension to learning and the changes in, initially, the children's behaviour and then of course their learning in the classroom.

This all was put in place very quickly, and of course in time it developed to include so many other projects that made, what then became 'social learning', a part of every aspect of school life.

2. Leading through dialogue - talking and listening

A key part of leading a *social learning agenda*, is that people are given the opportunity to discuss it. Any change results in questions as one seeks to understand and test ideas out. But, in the same way, change also results in answers, as one comes up with meanings and solutions. The role of the leader is to recognise this and to allow that need for dialogue.

JF: Head teachers - this is a message for you:

Much has been written about the nature and style of leadership and the characteristic, qualities and attributes of leaders, to the point where there is indeed a high degree of consistency in the messages that are being dispatched and received, such as: the importance of having a clear vision, the need for passion and commitment and a focus on distributed leadership. However, little has been written about the precise nature of such vision nor the principles, beliefs and values that 'should' underpin a school's vision. Little has been written about the specific moral imperatives, other than raising attainment and preparing children for life in the 21st Century, and more recently on promoting British values, that should drive a school's vision. Even less has been written about the role of the child in the process other than a view often referred to as a 'holistic approach', which itself can be interpreted in a variety of ways.

It is exactly these kinds of themes that we need to be talking about in our schools. Questions like:

1. What ways of thinking are driving our approach to education?
2. Which values, do we as a learning community, believe should children be exposed to?
3. What role should children play in shaping this discourse around their learning?

These need to be topics of conversation as we catch up in the staff room, as we sit down with colleagues to do some planning, as we meet with parents. In these settings and more, leadership involves encouraging an atmosphere for such dialogue.

In the Executive Summary of a recent report from the National College of Teaching and Learning, 'Freedom to Lead: a study of outstanding primary school leadership in England' (Mathews et al, 2014), the word 'pupil' only appears once and the word 'learning' is notable by its absence. Although there are some positive suggestions, the document maintains a view of the adult-child relationship as one in which the head teacher sits on top of a pyramid and which promotes a model of dialogue in which children are simply invisible.

Senior Leader

Children

However, if we are to establish a model of leadership that allows a vision for change to fully thrive, then surely this model needs to alter as the voice of all members of that learning community are acknowledged.

Children

Senior Leader

It means that one of the roles of a leader is to put themselves in places where such dialogue can happen. An article called 'Enchanted Head Teachers' (Woods, 2002) continues to influence my attitude to leadership at a number of levels. Included as one of its headings is 'I got caught teaching; closeness to children'. It is so easy for head teachers to shut themselves away in the office as we undertake more and more of the paperwork. But opportunities to be in the classroom or in the lunch hall all provide opportunities for dialogue that are essential to furthering an effective social learning community. Indeed, one of my favourite places for dialogue was on the playground as parents dropped off and picked their children up from school. Outside of my office parents were far more open to talk!

Balancing administration, management, leadership, children's learning and all those other demands that a head teacher faces is not easy. However, just to make sure that I never got these out of proportion I would keep a diary that I would complete every Friday after school within which I had a single question 'What have I done this week that has had a direct impact on children's learning?'.

As a final thought it is important to recognise that encouraging dialogue does not mean that everyone has to agree. Another influential leadership article 'Maverick Heads' (Hay Group, 2002), includes as one of its headings 'make enemies'. I am not sure the aim should be to create enemies but rather to be prepared that any efforts to create change might result in enemies. This is something that we need to be aware of at whatever level of leadership we are engaged in. It is how we handle the fallout as a result of change that matters. As such those that disagree must know, perhaps even more than those that agree, that their views are important, that just because they might not accept an approach that does not mean that they will subsequently sit separate to the rest of the learning community. Good channels of communication must therefore be in place so that there is a way of sharing (not necessarily directly to you), that means that factions do not arise and that individual agendas do not impact on the emerging vision. From the point of view of the head teacher, they must have strategic overview and exploit opportunities; connecting theories and practices and although one should not seek to create enemies there is a place for professional challenge and meaningful discussion, especially where that leads to a greater understanding of learning.

Leadership must include creating opportunities for dialogue.

Case Study - Parent Power - School 1 - Leading a Dialogue:

Parent Power - School 1, was John's second headship. It was perceived by children, parents, staff, governors and the Local Authority as a good school. For John it was a school reflected in the following statement, one 'full of passive and compliant learners who were being offered a restricted uninspiring curriculum that wholeheartedly focused on academic attainment'.

The challenge for John was to 'refocus' the school without losing the support of the staff, governors and probably more importantly, due to the context of the school, the parents. To make the point; at his first parent's meeting, which focused on the teaching of reading, there was standing room only.

JF: **The parents had not come to find out about reading they had come to find out about me! Here was an opportunity I could not lose and it gave me a chance, very early on, to explore themes such as; the importance of self confidence, self esteem, self regulation, the precursors to effective learning. The evening was very quickly followed up by letters home which gave me a way in to start the 'refocusing' process.**

3. Leading through personal development - keep on learning

Learning at school is not just for the children.

JF: When I reflect on all that has influenced me during my career I remember all I have learnt from the courses I have taken, the academic papers I have read, the colleagues I have worked alongside from the deputy heads that have questioned my thinking to the NQT's that have brought fresh perspectives and of course the children. Some of those I could list by name, others might have simply sparked a thought through a passing comment. However, it was a hunger for me to learn and continue learning as a leader, that gave these encounters particular meaning.

It is an attitude that needs to be encouraged at every level of a school community. However, this is something that can be encouraged by the senior leadership team through a desire to establish professional learning communities. A professional learning community must start with an individual examining their attitude towards what they do each day. Do you just turn up and hope the day goes quickly? Or is there a real sense of pride and with it doubt in what you do and how you do it, as you strive to do it as well as you can? Leadership can provide an environment in which the individual strives to further their skills as a learner (whether child or teacher), one that needs to be grounded on a sense of trust and collegiality (see for example Education Scotland, 2009), where a personal ambition becomes a collective ambition for change and excellence.

This will be extended in relation to Action Research - later in this chapter.

From a personal point of view, as part of my journey as a leader I reflected a lot on the following mind map (which makes sense to me – I hope to you). It reminded me of not only what I needed to do but also those areas where I needed to develop or encourage others to develop.

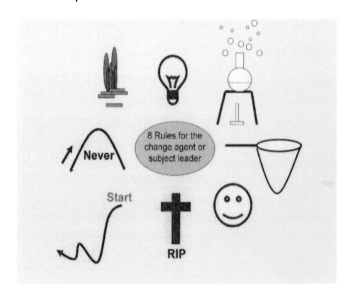

1. Starts Fires: challenge to create an urgency and desire for change. (From the flame and move round clockwise)
2. Have a bright idea and a friend.
3. Take Risks: a willingness to experiment and innovate.
4. Capture the moment: recognise, acknowledge and value the positive successes.
5. Be optimistic.
6. Nurture aliveness: is everyone okay - well-being is important for all.
7. Establish a common starting point: change must begin where the school staff are.
8. Never work uphill: look for short term gains, take small steps.

For me these remain a guide as I consider leadership with senior staff, NQT's, support staff and the children.

Personal development is an important part of leadership. Change will not happen unless someone believes it can.

A Professional Learning Community: JF: The key, as far as I am concerned, is that if a head teacher is serious about change, then establishing a professional learning community is necessary. Change does not happen overnight.

'Do the difficult things while they are easy and do the great things while they are small. A journey of a thousand miles must begin with a small step'. It is a phrase from the writings of the Ancient Chinese philosopher Lao Tzu and provides a realistic starting place for any journey that involves change. Change in schools is never easy. Schools have a particular way of doing things, as we have seen in previous sections: a method that is shaped by time, space and the required targets that are placed on school as an institution.

But despite these restrictions that are defined by school governors, local policy and directives from the Department of Education and so on, head teachers do still have room to make choices! As does the teacher in the classroom!

It is as a result of those choices that those first steps can be made. Establishing a *social learning agenda* in your school is not going to happen overnight, therefore as one seeks to get going, one needs to be realistic and identify those first small steps.

JF: Since we have begun to share the *social leaning agenda*, we have encouraged schools to undertake a social learning audit, to find out what they are already doing in relation to social learning and what scope there is for further development. The targets at the start of each of these chapters reflect the questions on which we have based an assessment of schools. It is by asking such questions that it becomes clear which pillars need to be the focus of attention, as a plan is put in place that recognises that it is not possible to do everything at once. Setting yourself goals based on an assessment of where you are and therefore how you need to change, will help you to focus your resources and invest time in the most needed areas. It is a process that demands engaging with vision, dialogue and personal development (as discussed above) and offers a platform through which to encourage the ambitions of a 'leader of change' within the context of creating a professional learning community.

Example from Practice: Democratic Schools

The hierarchical nature of schools has meant that change in the past has been seen as a narrowly managed process. Change is defined by the policy makers, this is then passed on to the school leaders and then that change is imposed. Change in schools does not need to be defined in this way. An exciting example of 'change' in schools is presented by the so called democratic schools. What these schools do, drawing off the theories of John Dewey and others, is recognise the extent to which school is constantly changing. That change does not need to be initiated necessarily by a policy maker, but could just as easily be presented by a child. These schools have developed a structure that allows them to have ideas expressed, but also to react to them. Here the traditional 'leader' is not defined in terms of their 'power' but for the more subtle qualities needed to facilitate a dynamic community, one that requires level of trust and respect if it is to flourish.

Strategies for leading change

It is absolutely key that change is focused on facts. Yes, the vision is important but part of making that vision visible so that it sticks, is demonstrating the impact (or not) of change. This is particularly important in relation to the *social learning agenda*, for as we have explored in earlier sections, assumptions have dominated so much of the way in which we have come to engage with children. Rather than simply assuming that we as adults have the answers, it is important that we encourage change based on 'research' in a variety of forms.

The following section looks at the role of:
- action research,
- coaching,
- children as leaders

These models fit well within efforts for a *social learning agenda*. Once you have established your vision, coaching then becomes a useful way of building and developing that vision. However, as we keep repeating, it is an approach that is increasingly effective when children are involved.

Action research:

JF: Action research and/or teacher led development work is in its heyday and the move towards 'evidenced based practice' is developing at a fast pace. So what is action research? Carson and Sumara's (1997) define it using these three criteria. An inquiry that:

1. seeks to learn about the complexly formed, ecologically organised relations of lived experience,
2. is specifically organised around questions of learning, understanding and/or interpretation,
3. self-consciously attempts to alter perception and is transformational in nature.

In short to me this means,

a. Is the classroom research going to take into account the complex issues associated with learning?
b. Is the research going to be driven by an understanding of learning?
c. Are we willing to transform what happens in the classroom?

A report by the BERA-RSA (British Educational Research Association and Royal Society for the Encouragement of the Arts) Inquiry identified a number of benefits that can be the result of action based research. This study found that as a result of an action research approach teachers were more informed by the latest relevant research and that the school environment encouraged and supported 'research literacy'. It also showed that there was an increase in personal and collective professional responsibility and that the definition and nature of professional development changed, leading to 'multiple opportunities'.

These opportunities have to be managed by the school otherwise there is a danger that developments can become ad hoc and stray from the main messages, rationale and/or purposes within the school. It is also interesting to note that action research does not have to be formal and add to the teachers work load. In its simplest form, teachers can consider which issue they feel needs to be addressed within their classrooms in terms of effective teaching and learning. Collaborative discussions can lead to small scale developments. Teachers can then trial, test and feedback to colleagues in terms of impact and obstacles. This cycle can then be repeated. When one of my staff encountered a more formal approach to action research, they suddenly said to me "isn't that what we have been doing?". Of course the answer was yes; surely the notion and importance of reflective practice is a key element of being a professional.

This environment for research should be part of what happens in the classroom, whether in a formal or less formal way. Here are some questions that may help you in considering the role of research in your learning community.

1. What is my understanding of 'research'?
2. What skills, attributes and characteristics do I need?
3. What level of motivation and self-confidence is driving my research? Is it sustainable?
4. Have I the skills, time and support to be an effective researcher?
5. What assumptions, beliefs and/or ideology underpin my research?
6. How informed am I by the latest relevant research?
7. What connections do I have with the wider research community?
8. Have I read and embraced conflicting, contradictory or critical reviews?
9. How 'open-minded' is my approach?
10. How broad are my horizons? Am I looking beyond my declared intentions, proposed outcomes and success criteria?
11. When evaluating, how 'authentic, accurate and reliable' are my findings'?
12. Can I draw out generalisations from my findings?

Case Study School - Time to Change: School 2 - John's thoughts on implementing action research

JF: This was particularly apparent to me in School 2. It was a community that had for so long been under the hammer of the local education authority. The result was a never-ending struggle to reach the required levels of accountability. In this context no one was questioning why they were doing what they were doing, they were just doing it. What these strategies encourage is a growing personal responsibility for practice, one that acknowledges formal accountability but is not defined by it.

It is difficult to envisage action research being effective if it were not in the context of seeking to create a professional learning community. However, it could be argued that by embarking on a programme of action research this contributes to the development of a professional learning community. This is exactly what we did in School 2; in fact we did not even use the term action research we just did it!

There is no doubt that I have learnt much from reading Sue Annis Hammond's book entitled *The Thin Book of Appreciative Inquiry*. It seemed to hit home, especially in a school where very little had been appreciated in the past. Two strands moved us forward.

First, in a school where little had been previously valued and where there was significant external accountability it was important for all the staff to realise and appreciate that 'some' of what was going on was at least good. As a result we looked at those children who were being successful, who were making progress, who were demonstrating at least age related expectations and asked the question why? The review clearly showed that the issues related to self. The successful children were more confident, had greater self esteem, were willing to take risks, sought external rewards than those who were less successful. Sharing this view gave greater impetus to moving forward with our *social learning agenda*. In the first place initiated by myself but more importantly recognised as important by the rest of the staff. A very simple strategy we used was;

DREAM: what potential do children have that we are not tapping into

DARE: let's take a risk, 'rethink' and just have a go

DELIVER: let's trial something

DIFFERENCE: what impact was there

Second, we embarked on a journey of 'action research' but not initially in a formal way. We embraced research by dropping in relevant academic articles into the staffs' pigeon holes, made time in staff meetings for discussion and caught 'staff in the corridors looking for champions'. We did formally change the schools' motto from 'the spirit to succeed' which I did endorse to 'a learning community with the spirit to succeed'. Over time we did encourage staff to keep a learning log and/or a portfolio of evidence outlining their journey. This ensured that teachers were confident when sharing their 'research'. Staff decided on their own focus and eventually we did develop a library of success.

Trust and respect does take time to build, however. Let me give you an aside. One of my staff suffered from low self esteem and a lack of confidence; and as a result, her teaching was not of the best. This was in part due to the negative feedback that she had been given over a long period of time. However, at the same time she had a great desire to improve and was very committed to the school. As part of her professional development I suggested that she video record herself teaching. My advice was to record the whole lesson but only focus on ten minutes of it when reviewing, which the teacher did. I then asked if she wanted to share it with me, she was happy to do so. We watched the video together and exchanged views and ideas. I then took the next step and suggested that we show the extract to the whole staff. She and I scripted and agreed a fifteen minute presentation about what we were both going to say. When the day came, the video was shown, explored and discussed. At the end of which there was spontaneous applause. What more do I need to say, other than videoing and peer coaching became a very important aspect of the school's continued professional development provision.

Coaching - furthering a professional learning community:

JF: I always remember a member of staff saying to me "John just tell us what you want us to do and we will do it". This has stayed with me as a reminder of balance; some staff do want to be told, others want mentoring, others seek advice and many over time will embrace coaching. The key for a leader is knowing 'which' and 'when'.

Keen and Eager School 3 - has been developing a *social learning agenda* for more than 18 months. The school has the Agenda fixed within its vision and development plan for the school. Social Learning is visible in many spaces throughout the school, but in order to develop what is going on in the classroom, the next step is to celebrate what has been successful and to support others in developing it in the context of their own group of children.

It is through a model of coaching, based on Sir John Whitmore's (2009), GROW model, that this was advanced. What this model encourages is:

- To explore what they want to achieve in terms of goals to improve learning.
- To look through different lenses' in terms of the realities as perceived by the pupils, parents and staff.
- To consider a range of options.
- To decide what actions to take.

For Keen and Eager School 3, coaching provided a good next step as part of building a professional learning community, which was focused on creating a true spirit to succeed. Coaching is, therefore, an empowerment model that can be used in a range of ways to support management of behaviour as a learning strategy, or simply as a tool to build confidence. The following case study outlines in a little more detail the way in which we used the GROW model in School 3.

Case Study - Keen and Eager - School 3 - Coaching

As part of advancing the Social Learning Agenda and supporting all staff (and children) to engage with it as part of everyday practice in the classroom, Keen and Eager have embraced a school wide coaching model. The programme has seen staff trained up in coaching and then supported in sharing those skills with others. These will then be passed on to the children.

To support staff in pursuing their community defined goals, the model has evolved to be combined with certain learning vehicles, in this case Edward de Bono's 'thinking' hats (2016) (discussed more in the following chapter).

So as the coach and coachee pursue:

G oal

- What do you want to achieve?

- What would achieving this lead to long term?

- When would you like to achieve this by?

R eality

- What is the current position?

- What stops you from moving on?

O pportunities

- What could you do?

- What else?

- What else?

- and what else?

W ill

- What will you do?

- What will be the first step?

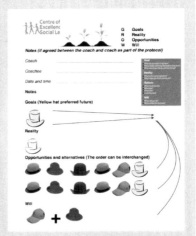

These become linked to thinking hats. Encouraging the coach and coachee to think about the opportunities that way of 'thinking' might add to the task and integrating this into everyday practice.

Once this has been tested by the teachers it will then be passed on to the children.

Children as leaders:

Mentoring: Coaching is a model that can easily be developed with children as well as adults, as can action research. Stephen Covey's *Leader in Me* (2008) is a great example of how language that is more often at home in the boardroom can become part of the conversation in the classroom, used by adults *and* children. Covey's leadership model, is a useful starting point for equipping children so that they can be more involved in this process of change.

Time for Change - School 2 looked to adapt Covey's model in collaboration with the children. In this project, the children were directly involved in exploring Covey's '7 habits' and in looking to make sense of them within the context of their learning community. This resulted in children then exploring ways in which those 'habits' could then be made use of and what their role could be as advocates for children as leaders.

Research Teams: School councils have often been relied on to provide children with an opportunity to have a voice. One of the problems with school councils, which is supported by research, is that children often feel that their participation is limited by the ongoing power dynamic that adults have over children. We have explored this through setting up child-run research teams.

Children were invited to apply. In the first instance those replies were considered by teachers; however, once we had the first group of children in post, from then on they reviewed applications and made decisions on recruitment. The children then received some training in how to research. They looked at the different types of research, through to the methods that they might use to gather their information. The children then considered topics to examine and then set about researching these.

The results were then shared widely throughout the community. They became a focus for examination by senior staff and governors and the children followed up on the recommendations they presented as they acted to bring about change.

Project Ownership: Keen and Eager - School 3 has seen children as leaders as a really important strand in developing attributes to support the *social learning agenda*. As such it has given children the opportunity to run their own clubs, for example, setting up a school newsletter and undertaking positions of responsibility through which they can offer guidance and support to other students.

Other ways in which we have seen schools encourage children as leaders is through:

- Welly walks: encouraging leadership (EYFS)
- Outdoor learner/ Explorers programmes (Years 1/2)
- Home and Away - Your Rights and Responsibilities (Years5/6)
- Job Shop (Key Stage 2)

This is an example of the template used to promote opportunities at the Job Shop

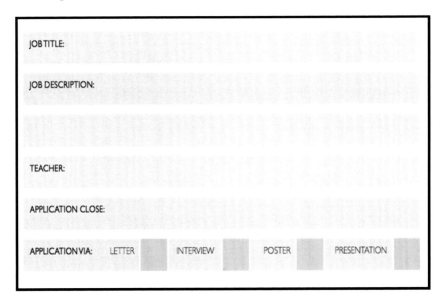

Conclusion

It is never going to be easy to bring about change. This chapter has tried to introduce some themes that might help to order your thinking as you pursue your vision for your learning community. Leadership is about championing a vision, but sharing it so that it develops in partnership with others.

JF: A leader, therefore, whether a child or adult must:
- Have the space to have an idea
- Have the opportunity to develop that idea
- Be encouraged to be reflective
- Have access to relevant knowledge and skills
- Be able to collaborate
- Be allowed to think 'win win'!

This chapter reflects the extent to which an adult leader in a social learning community should be focused on developing those relationships to maximise the learning opportunities for each individual child. Essentially, change is created by having an idea, talking and listening and being prepared to keep on learning. The managerial language that often accompanies discussions around leadership should not get in the way of us recognising that it is all about being a good facilitator, a role that only works if one recognises the softer (but often harder) side of leadership that comes with building relationships.

Remember change is not good enough, transformation is what is required and this can only be achieved by a learning community working together. Leadership is therefore required at every level.

Creating Change - Lead:

- What opportunities are there in your school for children to 'act' as leaders?
- What skills do the children need to have to be effective leaders?
- What opportunities are there for all members of staff to 'act as leaders'?

Building block 4 – *speak*: compose a language for social engagement

Introduction

	Social Learning Aims	Pillar Four: Speak	Principles or Drivers
The Social Learner	Allowing the individual child to grow in their awareness of themselves and others.	Speak: compose a language for social engagement	Children develop a language through which to 'define' their learning and relationships
			A defined list of social learning characteristics
	Equipping children with knowledge and skills so that they can successfully navigate the complexities of the social world they are part of.		Ability to recognise, understand and engage with vehicles for learning across the school
			Strategic plan for building and developing a language of engagement (learning, relationships and participation)
	Providing a foundation to maximise the child's learning potential in school and to increase children's participation and engagement in their families and communities.		Children equipped with language through which to express and share their own feelings and engage with the feelings of others.

You don't need to look far to find examples that show some of the challenges we face if we are not speaking the same language and I don't mean foreign languages, simply the complications that can arise in our own language. Think of the three knights who heard King Henry III say "who will rid me of this turbulent priest", which led to the murder of Thomas À Becket in Canterbury Cathedral. Was the King being rhetorical or was he giving an order? Fast forward to today; how hard is it to come up with a similar example, perhaps from a politician, whose words might have a particular meaning to them but which might be understood in a slightly different way by others? The need to clarify the supposed meaning held by language is not restricted to the subtlety of adult conversation, rather children are very aware of it too. Not only does this form part of children's daily interactions, it surrounds them in other forms for example through story telling. Those of us who are frequent visitors to the Island of Sodor will know very well that Thomas the Tank Engine and friends are constantly having to deal with the misunderstandings that arise through the use of language, and the 'confusion and delay' that results.

Schools, like all other areas of society, have a language of their own. A friend and I would joke about listening to our wives talk (both primary school teachers): the words they used and the way they talked meant that only other teachers, and notably other teachers from the same school, would fully understand what they were speaking about. The challenge for schools is that there is such a variety of vocabularies in play. From the range of vocabularies brought by the children, which increases with the number of foreign languages spoken, to the administrative language of the office, the supervisory language of the playground, the interactive language of the children, the language of the older teachers, the language of the newer teachers, the language of the senior leadership team, the language of the governors, the language of the parents and so on. So many different people with very different ways of talking about the same subject. The result, perhaps not surprisingly, is that communication is not always as effective as we might hope, with the result that misunderstanding inevitably leads to 'confusion and delay'!

The social in language:

Interaction is fast and furious in school. Children facing different people, different contexts - all day long. There is a lot to take in. Here is not the place to go into expansive detail about the role of language in learning, there are plenty of others who have done this as they focus on questioning and oracy, getting to grips with reading and writing, thinking about the non-verbal and the ability to listen (Pollard, 2014) and the list could go on. All of this is very important and forms a very real part of a child's school day, but how much of it is focused on providing a common or shared language through which all members of a learning community can engage in supporting the social learner? A consequence of Hattie's (2009, 2012) call for visibility in learning (considered in the last chapter) has for us resulted in the need to ask questions about how we seek to 'talk' about this social dimension to learning.

Many educationalists talk about the importance of scaffolding. Scaffolding suggests that teachers create a frame that helps to pull together the learning that takes place, and it offers a structure within which that learning can happen effectively. A starting point for us, therefore, is to have a language through which social learning can take place, which is accessible to all who are part of that learning community. Notably, this vocabulary will vary to different extents between different communities, but what is important is that it is identified, defined, used and understood. Language is thus a key component of the *social learning agenda*, as it offers a common vocabulary through which children (and adults) can take up their place in the community as they access and engage with their learning.

Developing a shared vocabulary

The following section draws together themes from earlier 'pillars' as it presents a comprehensive approach to establishing a language for social engagement. Approaches to language can be reflected in more specific projects, but here the focus is on how ethos, community and leadership can come together as a school establishes a vocabulary that allows the social dimension of learning to be visible, explicit and practical.

To help offer an idea of what this looks like in practice we are going to focus the practical examples around Keen and Eager - School 3. We will discuss how some of the other schools engaged with this at the end of the chapter.

Step 1 - The social learner:

This book began by making a simple statement - that the point of school is to establish the child as a social learner. It is, therefore not surprising, that if a language for social engagement is the aim, this must begin with a recognition and acknowledgement of the child as a 'social learner' (you can remind yourselves of our definition from the table at the start of this chapter).

Step 2 - Be clear and explicit about your ethos:

Strap-lines are everywhere and schools are no exception. School strap-lines come to offer a sense of their ethos, their mission. But are they just words or do they really mean something? If those words mean something, who do they mean something to and how then is this applied within that learning community?

Keen and Eager - School 3 had a strap-line. It was a good strap-line, the teachers knew it and the children knew it. As I was being taken round the school for the first time, my two young guides told me how important this strap-line was as "it is the starting point for our school". "Great" I responded, "so what does it mean"? This question was a little harder to answer. The children knew what the strap line of the school was but not what it meant. Indeed it was not just the children, for the staff too knew the strap line but they didn't know the meaning. Without understanding the ethos and being able to verbalise it, it cannot be applied.

JF: In so many of my schools, the ethos has been something that has been in place for some time. The school may have spent a fair bit of money getting their strap line printed onto their headed paper, maybe onto a name plaque that sits outside of the school and even chiselled onto windows. This does not mean that first, it should not be questioned and second, that it should not be added to or indeed changed. Here, change can be done in a sensitive way. This might mean adding to an existing strap line: in School 2 I added the words 'a learning community' to the existing words 'spirit to succeed'. It might however, just mean trying to understand or make sense of what a strap line, which has been around for some time, really means. It is about finding the right words through which your ethos can form part of the dialogue within your learning community.

Step 3 - Identify 4 or 5 value based words (linked to your defined ethos) that capture what you are about:

Educationalists Bill Lucas (2005) and Guy Claxton (2002) unwittingly started a game in schools over what core words schools might use in defining themselves and their curriculums. Both Lucas' and Claxton's ideas (some might say rather unimaginatively) take on a very similar form as they pursued words beginning with 'R'.

Resourcefulness
Remembering
Resilience
Reflectedness
Responsiveness
(Lucas 2005)

Resilience
Resourcefulness
Reflectiveness
Reciprocity
(Claxton, 2002)

Of course the serious point behind these was that schools could use them to help frame a common language from which learning could take place. It is a really useful model, within which a few core words provide the basis for a language of learning that can then be communicated throughout a school community. However, neither Claxton nor Lucas engaged with the fact that there does not necessarily need to be uniformity in the language that schools use. There are many value based words that can effectively help to frame a school's approach: what is important is for a school to pick words that mean something for them, and then to carefully share that meaning with their users.

In 'Time for Change - School 2' this saw the school picking six key words that could be used to capture and explore their mission statement (they just happened to be words beginning with 'R').

In 'Keen and Eager - School 3', the school had inherited a strap-line and it was the words from that strap line that then became the key words that were to be used within the community, as part of communicating and engaging in *their* learning ethos. This is explored in detail below.

What is important is for schools to find words that allow them to start to discuss their ethos, otherwise the strapline is nothing more than a clever phrase that sits in a small box at the top of a school newsletter.

Step 4 - Place these words in the context of a learner in your school:

Okay, great so we have a mission statement that places the social learner at the heart of the learning community and we have defined our value based words, which are ready to be applied to the children's learning. But isn't this still all a bit abstract? What does this really look like on a Tuesday afternoon when we go swimming or in a literacy lesson on a Friday morning? Well, it works a little bit like this. So far we have been constructing the different parts of a framework to allow the social learner to thrive. We started with a general definition of the 'social learner' but are now moving to what that might look like in your particular learning community. What is important to realise here is that although we might all strive for children to be 'social learners', the way in which we reach that goal will be, and should be, different in every school community.

It is important to say one more time, that the following illustration is not something that you can just copy and apply. It is specific to a learning community.

In Practice - Keen and Eager - School 3 - Speak!: In 'Keen and Eager - School 3', the school had inherited a strap-line which was:

'Have faith, take responsibility, show respect and achieve'

It was something that had been considered and reviewed only shortly before a new leadership team took over. Changing the strap line was going to be hard. In any case, the strap line had the potential to communicate the ethos that the school was now looking to share. (Indeed this is the case for many schools, a strap-line is something that is inherited, it has grown and developed with the school and although there may be a little wiggle room, add a word here and there changing it entirely is not always practical). However, what could be considered was the meaning attached to the words in the strap-line, 'faith', 'responsibility', 'respect' and 'achieve'.

How were these words going to be interpreted within the context of the new ethos that the school was setting itself? To make sense of these words and to find a way in which they could have application on the children's journey of learning, the community as a whole needed to be engaged in making sense of these words and in framing their meaning. These steps (as stated earlier) offer a model that starts to look like this:

Keen and Eager School 3 - composing language - steps 1to 3

The Social Learner (step 1)	School Ethos (step 2)	Value Based Words (step 3)
➢ a child growing in awareness of themselves and others,		Faith
➢ a child equipped with the knowledge and skills so that they can successfully navigate the complexities of the social world they are part of,	Have faith, take responsibility, show respect and achieve	Respect
		Responsibility
➢ a child given a foundation to maximise their learning potential AND opportunities to increase their participation and engagement in their families and communities.		Achieve

The next step, step 4, is to think about how these words can be broken down so that they can have application to children's everyday learning.

In 'Keen and Eager - School 3' the children started off by taking the value based words and looking at them in classes. They created posters and made films as they sought to make sense of what these words meant and how they might apply to their learning.

These posters were then shared with all adults who were part of the community. Like the children they were asked to think about what these words meant.

Based on this dialogue, key phrases emerged (which are detailed below) which became a focus for defining what this might look like in the classroom.

And so the table opposite evolves as step 4 is included (see next page).

The Social Learner (step 1)	School Ethos (step 2)	Value Based Words (step 3)	Definition of Value Based Words (step 4)
➢ a child growing in awareness of themselves and others, ➢ a child equipped with the knowledge and skills so that they can successfully navigate the complexities of the social world they are part of, ➢ a child given a foundation to maximise their learning potential AND opportunities to increase their participation and engagement in their families and communities.	Have faith, take responsibility, show respect and achieve	Faith	Belief
			Love
			Courage
			Trust
		Respect	Value
			Selflessness
			Empathy
			Tolerance
		Responsibility	Ownership
			Choices
			Motivation
			Reliability
		Achieve	Resourcefulness
			Confidence
			Resilience
			Personal Goals

Step 5 - Link these words directly to the curriculum:

Yes, the next step is to link the attributes to the curriculum (in its broadest sense applying to all aspects of school). Having a clear list of learning characteristics or attributes which one is aiming for within a learning community offers all members a very definite starting point for engaging with social learning. As has been commented on earlier, one of the biggest challenges in this area has been the fact that the social dimension to learning has been seen as invisible, something that just happens. Here it is made explicit, here it is made visible and it is then for those who facilitate children's learning to work out where within the curriculum, in its widest sense, they can create the opportunities for children to engage with these characteristics and grow in their ability to master them.

Keen and Eager School 3 - composing language - steps 1 to 5

The Social Learner (step 1)	School Ethos (step 2)	Value Based Words (step 3)	Definition of Value Based Words (step 4)	Learning Attributes (step 5)	
As in previous tables	As in previous tables	Faith	Belief Love Courage Trust	Faith in Myself	Link Christian and British values to my life
					Think about what I believe
					Consider others' beliefs
					Be brave and accept mistakes
				Faith in Others	Rely on others
					Develop trusting relationships, including making friends
		Respect	Value Selflessness Empathy Tolerance	Respect for Self	Consider things that are important to me
					Belong to a school community
				Respect for Others	Keep an open mind and appreciate others points of view

					Understand the feelings of others
					Recognise things that are important to others
					Be generous and helpful
					Be courteous
		Respons-ibility	Ownership Choices Motivation Reliability	Manage Myself	Develop economic well-being skills
					Organise myself
					Keep myself safe
					Recognise and make healthy choices
					Understand rights and responsibilities
					Recognise and manage changes
					Recognise and name my feelings
					Manage my emotions and make positive decisions
				Managing with Others	Develop leadership
					Recognising and use strategies for managing pressure and persuasion from others

					Respond to risky or negative relationships, such as bullying, and ask for help
		Achieve		Learning to Learn	Ready to learn
					Resilient: being ready, willing and able to lock on to learning
					Reflective: being ready, willing and able to become more strategic about learning
			Resourceful ness Confidence Resilience Personal Goals		Resourceful: being ready, willing and able to learn in different ways
					(Interdependent) Reciprocal: being ready, willing and able to learn alone and with others
				Effective Learning	Engagement: creating and thinking critically
					Motivation: active learning
					Thinking: playing and exploring

Step 6 - Ensure that learning vehicles are in place to allow children to engage with this language for learning in a way that is appropriate for them:

JF: Once learning communities have an idea of what they are working towards, it is then helpful to identify some 'vehicles' or learning strategies to help to give these learning attributes a place in the classroom. Learning strategies that I have used, and now encourage other schools to use that allow teachers to engage with that language for social learning within the day to day include Edward de Bono's (2016) hats and Kathleen Butler's (1998) learning styles.

Edward de Bono's hats can be used in a variety of different ways. For example, they can be used as a framework to help children and midday supervisors reflect on acceptable behaviour out on the playground:

White hat (facts):	What happened, keep to the facts?
Red hat (feelings):	How do the different individuals feel – before, during and now after the incident?
Yellow hat (benefits):	What would they have liked to have happened?
Black hat (cautions):	What obstacles or challenges do we have to overcome?
Green hat (creativity):	What ideas and actions can we think of to overcome?
Blue hat (process):	Agree amongst those involved what will be done?

Kathleen Butlers learning styles can also be used. Using different characters which help, especially young children, to explore the meaning and importance of skills associated with analytical, systematic, pragmatic, divergent and personal learning.

Case Study - Keen and Eager - School 3 - Implementing Butler's Ideas

The starting point of this approach began in the EYFS (Early Years Foundation Stage). We compared the characteristics of effective learning, as contained within the statutory guidance, with the key tenets of Kathleen Butler's work. The outcome of which was a list of learning attributes that children in the EYFS should be exposed to through the planned curriculum and used by the teachers in their conversations with the children; reaching a point where there was a common language used by both adults and children within the Early Years settings. This pilot was shared with all staff. The next step was for the whole school to look for a vehicle to explore this concept. History was chosen and a training day was provided. The focus was on split level objectives which identified and promoted not only relevant historical knowledge and understanding but also key learning attributes.

Conclusion

Here again are the six steps,

1. Acknowledge the social learner
2. Be clear and explicit about your ethos
3. Identify 4 or 5 value based words (linked to your defined ethos) that capture what you are about
4. Place these words in the context of a learner in your school
5. Link these words directly to the curriculum
6. Ensure that learning vehicles are in place to allow children to engage with this language for learning in a way that is appropriate for them.

These steps reflect a way of establishing a language of social engagement throughout school. However, the nature of this language, as we have said elsewhere will be specific to the learning community itself. Here, therefore, are some examples of what this process has looked like in some of the other schools we have worked in.

Case Study School Examples: A language for social engagement

In schools where this has been tested, the framework has helped to support curriculum coverage of the *social learning agenda*, ensuring that there is a whole school approach and commitment which can only happen as a result of a shared language for engagement. It has helped to embed practice and importantly the way in which children are able to engage with and communicate their learning.

Case Study - Parent Power - School 1 - Learning Logs

JF: In 'Parent Power - School 1' we spent a lot of time agreeing on the key words that we used to illustrate or make meaning of 6 'R's that we had chosen. The aim of this was to develop the staff and children's knowledge, understanding and use of the key words that demonstrated the 6 'R's in action, rather than them just being able to quote the name of the R's, 'barking at print'. These ideas then became integrated into learning logs that the children used.

The aim of the learning logs was to give the children the chance to reflect on certain learning attributes by highlighting examples from their own learning and then setting themselves targets.

Here is an example (taken directly form a learning log used in School 1):

Core Value Word: Resourcefulness
Resourcefulness means you know what to do when you get stuck. The learner who is resourceful knows where to go for help, knows and tries different strategies to learn, solves problems and challenges. They also ask very good questions to support their learning.

Learning Attributes:
– risk taker - inquisitive – adaptable – inventive – curious
– willing to make mistakes – enjoys exploring different routes
– willing to change direction – can apply prior learning and experience

Your Examples:
Date   Description

Your ongoing targets:

Case Study - A Way Forward - School 5 - Hearing from Everyone

Here the school's ethos was captured in just two words 'care and achieve', however, little opportunity had been given to explore what these two key words meant, how they were going to be promoted, recognised or acknowledged. As its first step the school decided to use a training day to explore the staff's views. The comments were collected, grouped and then titled. As a result seven sub headings now supported the two key words and the seven subheadings had agreed descriptors that were shared with the children. The children then made classroom displays translating the descriptors or what are now termed as 'learning attributes' into contexts that were meaningful to them. As part of this development a number of pupil interviews and structured discussions from Year 1 to Year 6 were carried out and to find out if the children had an understanding of what they meant and their value. It was very impressive and evidenced how quickly a working knowledge of the learning attributes was achieved.

This model works. It creates a framework within which schools can start to break down a language to make the *social learning agenda* real. That language will be unique to that learning community, and will provide a foundation for social learning that can then flow through the different parts of every school day.

Creating Change - Speak:

1. Having read a number of case studies in the chapter above, can you draw specific ideas from them? If so, how can these be replicated within your own school?

2. Think about the language that children use to describe their learning; what words and phrases do you normally hear children say? What does this tell you about their understanding of the 'learning process'?

3. Think about the language that teachers use at staff meetings or during pupil progress meetings to describe children's learning? What does this tell you about how learning is perceived?

4. What language, words and phrases do you want children and teachers to use in their discussions with regard to social learning; what curriculum vehicles could be used to promote this language?

Building block 5 - a*ct*: initiate opportunities for social learning

Introduction

	Social Learning Aims	Pillar 5: Act	Principles or Drivers
The Social Learner	Allowing the individual child to grow in their awareness of themselves and others. Equipping children with knowledge and skills so that they can successfully navigate the complexities of the social world they are part of. Providing a foundation to maximise the child's learning potential in school and to increase children's participation and engagement in their families and communities.	Act: initiate opportunities for practice	Children have awareness and confidence to take control of their learning and relationships.
			A commitment to develop children's skills to participate and engage
			Children recognise their potential and feel empowered to act as valued members of the communities
			The boundaries to 'act' are not confined to school
			School actively promote opportunities for participation and engagement

You might have a very strong partnership ethos, have worked to establish a positive learning community, have leadership and language under control, but if there are no opportunities to give your social learners a chance to put it all into practice then the learning journey will be limited.

In our experience we know that schools think this social dimension to learning is important. However, the way it is often 'done' is through the adoption of particular programmes of learning that can be bolted on to the curriculum. Many of these projects are very exciting and offer some fantastic learning opportunities but they stop short of fully addressing all of the social and structural realities needed for lasting educational change. Programmes, therefore, such as Stephen Covey's *Leader in Me*, as well as projects such as P4C (Philosophy for Children) to name but two, provide part of the answer by providing opportunities for practising those learning attributes, but they do not offer a complete solution.

What we want to explore in this chapter is the need for the *social learning agenda* to be embedded *throughout* a learning community and through this to *constantly* provide opportunities for action. As part of this, targeted projects can help to raise the profile of particular attributes, and we will share some examples of these.

Activating the social learning agenda

It is important to have a plan.

In 'Slow and Steady - School 4', there was a desire to increase opportunities for social learning within the school, but this was not part of any strategic way of thinking and as a result, the projects they introduced were limited in their effectiveness. What they needed from the start was a plan. This is reflected in the illustration below.

Establishing a Plan - Illustration

The Social Learning Agenda in action: bringing together research and innovation in practice

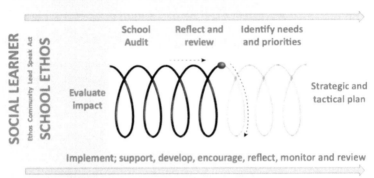

As part of encouraging schools to develop that plan for the *social learning agenda,* schools undertake a social learning audit. This was mentioned in a previous chapter, as was the fact that the questions that help to frame this audit appear at the start of each chapter. These questions therefore, form part of the steps highlighted in the table above, as communities look to form a strategic plan that can be evaluated and reviewed. This is not to suggest that each school needs a separate social learning plan (although it could), but rather those social learning steps come to form part of existing strategic thinking, for example, as part of school improvement plans.

JF: However, to shape the plan it is important to have a sense of where you might be going, as you develop steps that are unique to your learning community. The *social learning agenda* is focused on putting the 'plan' into action through the use of our curriculum model, illustrated below.

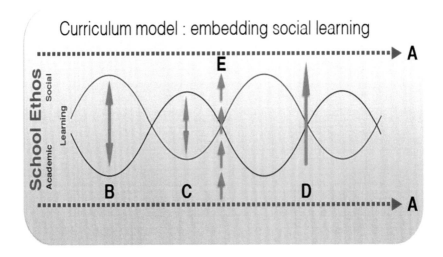

Curriculum model : embedding social learning

JF: The curriculum model invites schools to consider the activation of the *social learning agenda* through five component parts. These can then be directly defined and planned for as part of shaping opportunities for 'action'.

A. represents the whole school approach through the transmission of a shared ethos, highlighted for example, through a defined list of learning attributes, behaviour policies and whole school events such as assemblies.

B. represents any lesson within the curriculum; however, such lessons, through the use of 'split level objectives', weight a social learning target, such as developing an aspect of collaboration, as the priority. The learning activities reflect this.

C. represents any lesson within the curriculum; however, such lessons, through the use of split level objectives, weight an academic target, such as the rules of multiplication, as the priority. The learning activities reflect this.

D. represents projects with a whole school focus that seek to highlight defined learning attributes. These might be reflected in whole school projects on belonging, innovation and enterprise which will be interpreted differently for different year groups

E. represents additional project opportunities specific to year groups, for example an outdoor learning activity ran in Time for Change - School 2 that ran across years 1 and 2.

There is also an F and a G. These do not appear on the plan as it is, but reflect a sense of embracing community cohesion, as the *social learning agenda* is spread not only throughout school but beyond.

F. represents the ongoing focus on social learning in non-formal aspects of the children's school day, this would include approaches taken at, for example, play time and in the lunch hall.

G. represents the social learning that transcends the geographical boundaries of school and spreads into the wider learning community. This would include working with parents as well as engaging with members of the community such as local police officers and shopkeepers.

Projects in practice

Through the curriculum model, schools can then think about how to maximise opportunities for the social learner. This includes thinking about the way in which one goes about planning a lesson through to the way in which the playground is managed, opportunities for parents to be involved and much much more. The following diagrams reflect what are, in effect, 'fire starters', targeted projects that aim to ignite engagement with specific social learning attributes. They can also provide opportunities to engage adults and children in the different elements of the pillars that underpin the *social learning agenda*.

Targetted Projects - examples from Time to Change - School 2.

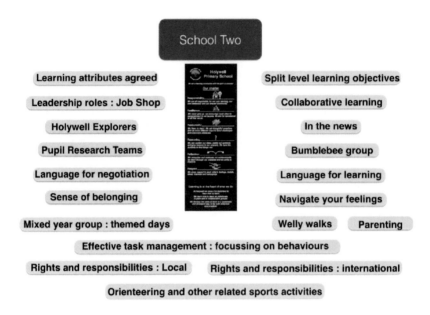

Targetted Projects - examples from Keen and Eager - School 3

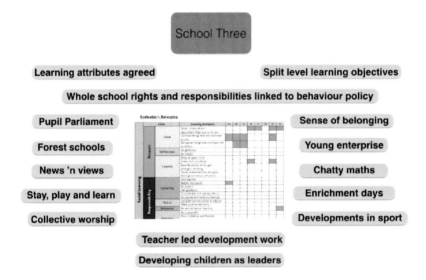

Case Study - A Way Forward - School 5 - Blogging your Log

In order to develop attributes around reflective learning, A Way Forward – School 5, set up learning logs, which the children were then invited to blog about. It offers an example of the way in which children can be invited to consider, review and share their learning. This is what some of the children shared on the blog:

'Thank you for coming up with the idea of the learning logs they are going to help me remember how much I've improved in my learning'.
'I think it is a better way for us to reflect on our learning'.
'I think they are really gonna help everyone in the class. They will help me remember what I have done previously in my learning'.

Note: we recognise the significant potential of technology to the *social learning agenda.*

As you can see these 'fire starters' for social learning in each of the case study schools are different. As such, they reflect not only the differences in the learning communities, but also in the interests and creativity of the staff. The model encourages personal and group initiative, but with the caution that any project needs to have

- a strategic focus
- a means for monitoring, evaluation and capture
- a desire to extend knowledge (research and practice)
- a stop button (recognising mistakes)

A strategic focus:

In the case study schools, successful projects emerged as a response to a defined drive to engage with particular social learning attributes. You will all know that there are lots of 'off the shelf' projects out there: projects that have already been developed and used and which can be tailored for exploring an aspect of a *social learning agenda*. The key part of using such projects, or projects of your own design, is that these need to be used strategically. Any project, whether one of those described above or an internationally successful scheme like 'Leader in Me', must be positioned within the wider context of your learning, as one creatively asks what 'attributes' will that project help the children to explore, as part of your community wide ambitions to support the 'social learner'.

A means of monitoring, evaluation and capture:

Whatever the size of a project, whether a whole school activity or a piece of work with a small group of children, the effectiveness of the enterprise can be supported by asking yourself some key questions, that will allow you to START as you mean to go on.

	Objectives	Tasks - to be reviewed at the start, middle and end of a project.
S	ocial learning goals	- What social learning attributes do you hope to address? - Why are these important? (this will help you to justify your need/ rationale for this project)
T	ime frame	- Realistic timetable: schools are busy places. Setting a time frame it allows those involved to more realistically manage the project and to work out how it needs to be prioritised in the context of other learning initiatives. - Dates in diary: defining dates allows all those involved to be clear on what each other's expectations are. We have learnt from experience not to underestimate how important this is. - A long term or short term project: do not be afraid to recognise that some projects take time.
A	ctivities	- Definable: What will this project look like? - Evolution: despite the effort we put in at the start of the project, we need to recognise that aspects of it may change.
R	esources	- Who: do you need to be involved in this project and what roles will you be looking for them to play? - What: do you need in order for this project to run (paper, footballs, outdoor equipment...)? - Where: does this project need to take place. Does it require a specific learning space? - How much: is this project going to cost?
T	argets	Impact and Influence: The implications this project has had on children's learning. Capture: How the data used to support the findings of this project are to be collected (pupil and staff journal, attainment targets, photos...) Dissemination: How and where will the findings of this project be shared? (a staff meeting, school newsletter, academic conference...)

113

The table below is an example of how the START model might look in the context of a real project. 'In the News' was a year 3 project, that developed to support children's engagement with both the language and opportunities for social learning.

	Objectives	Tasks - to be reviewed at the start, middle and end of a project.
S	ocial learning goals	- For children to grow in awareness of self and others - to equip with knowledge and skills to make a difference - to make the most of learning opportunities by: • developing a wider understanding of the world around us - both in relation to our immediate community and beyond (gaining a concept of 'local', 'national' and 'global' communities. • recognising and voicing one's own values and opinions • recognising and hearing the values and opinions of others • to reflect; ask thought provoking questions • to embed key skills for speaking and listening • to be able to identify and take positive actions
T	ime frame	In the News to take place weekly in each Y3 classroom. (time allocated decided by the teacher and flexible depending on nature of discussion/content of article i.e. debate/questioning/discussion & feedback in groups/whole class discussion). Not every session will be written up into a blog however, the learning reflections will be recorded as and when appropriate (children are to be part of this decision). July: Review blog entries and learning. Consider transition plan for year 2's coming up. Autumn: Project lead share at Senior Leadership Team meeting Spring: Review project plan Spring: Present ideas with video clips from children to a wider audience. Summer: Ready to be shared at regional meetings.

114

A	ctivities	At start up:
		⁻ Children respond to, share and collect thoughts on news worthy articles.
		⁻ Reflect on and discuss the content – introduce the idea of a moral dilemma/decision.
		⁻ Write up reflections into an online blog.
R	esources	⁻ Year 3 teachers to be responsible for finding time to plan.
		⁻ To use 'first news' as an initial source of identifying news stories.
		⁻ To create a framework though which the children can look to explore and manage their reactions to the stories that they look at.
T	argets	Impact and Influence: To measure the quality of questioning and the children's ability to reflect and empathise.
		Capture: The children's responses will be collected on a blog. Children will also be involved in reporting on their activities through the ideas captured on the framework.
		Dissemination:
		⁻ Sharing in the wider context of the school; through staff meetings and parent newsletters.
		⁻ To create blog buddies with international schools known to us.
		⁻ To share through local Teaching and Learning Alliance.

This project saw children, in the words of their teacher,

'gaining a deeper understanding of the world around them, as both international and more local issues are explored. They understand what it is to express an idea or opinion and are beginning to grasp what it means to discover a sense of self and voice, through using reasoning skills, presenting informed opinions.

As the children's thought process deepens we need to focus on their ability to express their thoughts through speech as they often struggle to be clear and concise'.

The START model offers a way of engaging with the elements of a project, such that a project can be reviewed and assessed as it develops.

Extend knowledge: linking research and practice:

There are so many creative ideas being developed within universities!

JF: There is so much innovation happening in our schools!

The key is to try and find ways to link the two. As we look to develop projects, it is therefore worth considering whether there is any relevant research that might support what you are trying to do.

Let me give you an example. You might have realised that despite your school council being a good idea it has only really provided a voice to those children who are already not shy in coming forward. It is restricted in the nature of the topics that it looks at and as a result it could be argued that it is merely tokenistic.

These were exactly the issues that Yamashita and Davies (2010) looked at as part of a project to increase children's participation in secondary school. What their work resulted in was a model that demonstrates how children's voices can be more effectively represented, as well as suggestions for possible headings for discussion which included children in engaging with those serious issues that really impacted their experiences. Notably, as part of this, they give the children the title 'professionals' as they acknowledge their value in offering insight and feedback, that can further practices within school (this links to the earlier discussion of research teams).

As such, in developing projects in Time for Change - School 2, we chose to send our project outlines to an external academic advisor, based at a university. They were asked to comment based on the following questions,

• General Reflection on Plans

• Relevant Academic Research and Writing

• Relevance to current Policy and Practice

It provided feedback that allowed teachers to help situate their creativity in school, with what was going on in the wider world. For some, this gave them the basis to write up their own academic articles as a means of sharing their projects, but also to contribute to this important cycle in which research and practice inform and re-inform each other.

A stop button:

JF: It is okay to not continue a project. We ran an idea that we called PAL (Personal Ambition Log). Upon reflection it sounded a little too much like pet food from the start! We tested it with children going swimming. In fact, in this particular context it worked really well. The children would identify a target to focus on before each swimming trip. They would then sit with a buddy on the bus and discuss their target for that week. After swimming, they sat with the same buddy and they discussed how they got on. The children then made a note of this - ready for setting a target for the next week. The problem was it was not quite ticking all the boxes. Yes it was okay, but was it a good investment of time and effort? Sometimes it is okay to say "stop". In fact, as a result we reviewed the idea and came up with something that we think is far stronger - we would not have done this if we had simply accepted a project that was only half working.

The project that PAL developed into is loosely called the Learning Wheel or Thought Wheel. What the wheel does is invite children to consider the relationship between taking on a task, the processes of that task, the challenges they might face in undertaking that task and how they might be able to overcome those challenges so that the task can be completed.

117

Conclusion

This wheel provides a fitting conclusion to this chapter.

Our 'learning wheel' or 'thought wheel' represents the dynamic and individual nature of learning: the voyage of discovery that we all go on whenever we take on a task. The way we are able to manage that journey affects how successful we are in completing our task. It is through engaging with the social dimension of us as people, that we realise how necessary it is to develop the knowledge and skills for navigating our journey through life. The social becomes, therefore the essence of successful learning. Attainment goals simply cannot be viewed outside of this dimension. Our aim in schools should not be to get children through their SATS, GCSE's, A-Levels or whatever exam a set of political administrators establish. It should be to create a hunger for learning that will see them strive to fulfil their own potential, both now and in the future. It should open up a world of opportunities and possibilities which they can follow as their passions and imaginations direct. Learning should not be defined by the answers that they give in a test but by the questions that they ask and their ability to investigate and explore the answers for themselves.

For there to be transformation in education then it must start by recognising the social dimension. A *social learning agenda* is about providing those opportunities, as adults seek to maximise the child's learning potential by giving them the chance to increasingly manage and shape their own learning journey.

Note: For more on the 'wheel' please do get in touch.

Creating Change - Act:

1. Having read the case studies and particularly having looked at the 'fire starter' projects, what ideas are relevant in your school? How could they be replicated?

2. What 'actions' could you START to help translate aspects of the *social learning agenda* into effective practice?

3. Has the proposed curriculum model relevance in your school? Consider how the different elements of the model - A, B, C, D, E, F, G are reflected in your practice?

Next steps

If you wish to undertake a journey of change in your school, the sections of this book should offer you not only some food for thought, but also some practical ideas that you can use.

Our *social learning agenda* has started to have an impact, as learning communities engage with this model.

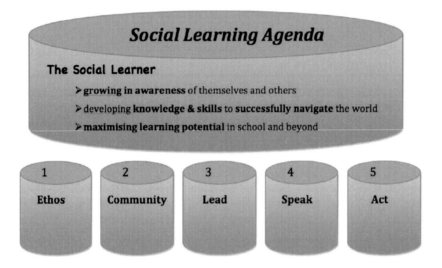

The pillars of Ethos, Community, Lead, Speak and Act in support of the Social Learner, provide a framework that can help you, not only think about approaches that can further children's learning potential, but also how to put this into practice.

As has been mentioned previously, each chapter started by introducing some principles or drivers: these can be used in order to examine how well your school is doing in relation to social learning. Asking these questions will give you a basis from which to work and a sense of what you need to focus on.

This book does not provide all the information or examples that we have; instead, it offers an introduction, from which you are invited to find out more. We are also building up information relating to:

- parents and the *social learning agenda*

- social learning and technology

- engaging children with additional needs

For information about how to contact us in relation to these issues and others please visit our website.

JF: Some closing thoughts...

Many of you may be thinking, well I enjoyed this book, but how will these ideas sit with Ofsted (or other regulatory bodies). Well, let me leave you with some extracts from Ofsted reports from three of our case study schools.

Case Study - Parent Power - School 1 - Extract from Ofsted Report
(following a number of years of using an early version of the *Social Learning Agenda*)

'...nurtures pupils' original ideas and personal qualities through all it does... A consistent focus on different, exciting ways of learning captures pupils' imagination very well so they really want to be in school. Many insist that they "like everything about it!"

Pupils have been fired with enthusiasm for understanding and for using the full range of skills involved in learning, thinking and drawing conclusions, so relish activities where these are put to the test in full.

The school values high standards not just in learning, thinking and academic work, but in personal development, so provides a rich variety of opportunities to foster different personal qualities...Many pupils have particular jobs to do in class or just volunteer happily to help teachers because this is part of the school culture, so all through the day children of all ages are part of a hive of activity. As one pupil stressed" there are a lot of responsibilities and I like to be kept busy."

Pupils' social and cultural awareness are fostered equally well through collaborative work, team-building activities... to deepen understanding of similarities and differences. Pupils value all their experiences.'

Case Study - Time for Change - School 2 - Extract from Ofsted Report
(following 1000 days of pursuing the *Social Learning Agenda*)

'...Behaviour is exemplary and relationships with staff are highly positive. Pupils are exceptionally polite, well mannered and motivated. They work well together to discuss ideas and support one another, particularly when pupils are newly arrived from other countries.

Pupils' excellent behaviour and positive attitudes to school make an outstanding contribution to their good learning and progress. Pupils are exceptionally keen to learn. They strive to give of their very best and work hard

One of the many strengths of this highly inclusive school is the way in which pupils from many different backgrounds work and play happily together. The 'Explorers' sessions where pupils engage in high quality, practical- learning activities in the school grounds support their collaborative learning experiences and encourage curiosity'.

Case Study - Slow and Steady - School 4 - Extract from Ofsted Report
(following growing engagement with the *Social Learning Agenda*)

The pupils' very positive attitudes to learning make a significant contribution to their excellent learning and rapid progress. Pupils of all ages are very keen to do well. They work hard at all times, listen carefully to their teachers and do their utmost to meet their expectations. The school is happy and harmonious because pupils conduct themselves very sensibly in lessons and at other times. They are very kind and considerate towards each other. Promoting the pupils' spiritual, moral, social and cultural development is at the heart of the work of the school. Pupils eagerly learn about values such as tolerance, respect for others and how to recognise right from wrong.

The first decision you have to make is whether or not you want to take the 'next step'. The challenge may seem daunting, the obstacles may seem high and difficult to overcome and the benefits may still seem a little unclear. However, I would ask you to consider why you entered into the teaching profession in the first instance, what drove you? Are those drivers still evident in what you say and what you do, or have they become a little lost in the passage of time? Let me urge you to take some quiet time and consider.

The five pillars have evolved over time, they stem from practice and what has worked well in my own schools and the ones we support. It is a way forward, a strategic approach.

The *social learning agenda* gives you the chance to make that difference to children's lives. It offers a chance for transformation that will not just see children succeed through reaching the latest attainment goals, but one that will give them a foundation that will serve them both now and into the future.

So is the next step worth taking?

Well if your desire is like ours, to maximise children's learning potential, then you have nothing to lose and everything to gain!

To find out about how we can help with:

- support your next steps
- children's engagement with the project
- becoming a social learning ambassador
- and more…

please visit our website

www.sociallearners.org

Bibliography

Astuto, T.A., Clark, D.L., Read, A-M., McGree, K. & Fernandez, L.deK.P. (1993). *Challenges to dominant assumptions controlling educational reform,* Andover, MA: Regional Laboratory for the Educational Improvement of the Northeast and Islands.

BERA (2014) *Research and the Teaching Profession: building the capacity for a self-improving education system British Educational Research Association,* London, England: British Educational Research Institution.

Bluebond-Langner, M. (1978) *The Private World of Dying Children,* Princeton, NJ: Princeton University Press.

Brighouse T, Woods P, (1999) *How to Improve Your School* London, England: Routledge.

Brooks, D. (2012) *The Social Animal: the hidden sources of love, character, and achievement,* Random House trade pbk. edn, New York, NY: Random House Trade Paperbacks.

Butler, K. (1998) *Learning and Teaching Style: In Theory and Practice,* Columbia, NY: Learning Dimension.

Cambridge Primary Review: R. Alexander (ed) (2010) *Children, Their World, Their Education, Final Report and Recommendations,* London, England: Rutledge.

Carson, T.R. & Sumara, D.J. (1997) *Action research as a living practice,* New York, NY: P. Lang.

Claxton, G. (2002) *Building Learning Power: helping young people become better learners,* Bristol, England: TLO.

Coles, M and Southworth, G. (eds) (2005) *Developing Leadership: creating the schools of tomorrow, professional learning,* Maidenhead, England: Open University Press.

Connolly, P. (1998) *Racism, Gender Identities and Young Children: social relations in a multi ethnic, inner city primary school,* London, England: Routledge.

Covey, S. R. (2008) *The Leader in Me: How schools and parents around the world are inspiring greatness, one child at a time,* New York, NY: Free Press.

Dahlberg, G. (2011) 'Policies in Early Childhood Education and Care: potentialities for agency, play and learning' In W. A. Corsaro, M.-S.

Honig & J. Qvortrup (Eds.), *The Palgrave Handbook of Childhood Studies*, Basingstoke, England: Palgrave Macmillan.

De Bono, E. (2016) [1987] *Six Thinking Hats,* Penguin Books, Middlesex, Enlgand: Harmondsworth.

Denham, S. A., Zinsser, K. M., & Brown, C. A. (2013) 'The Emotional Basis of Learning and Development in Early Childhood' In B. Spodek, & O. Saracho (Eds.), *Handbook of Research on the Education of Young Children* (3rd ed.). New York, NY: Lawrence Erlbaum.

Donaldson, M. McGarrigle, J. (1975) 'Conversation Accidents', *Cognition*, (3) 34, 1-50.

Donaldson, M. Hughes, M. (1979) 'The Use of Hiding Games for the Studying Co-ordination of Viewpoints', *Educational Review*, 31 133-40.

Dweck, C. (2006) *Mindset,* London: Constable and Robinson

Education Scotland (2009) *Learning Together: improving teaching, improving learning the roles of continuing professional development, collegiality and chartered teachers in implementing Curriculum for Excellence*, Livingstone, Scotland: HM Inspectorate of Education.

Etheridge, S. (2004) "Do You Know You Have Worms on Your Pearls?" Listening to Children's Voices in the Classroom', in P. Pufall and R. Unsworth (eds) *Rethinking Childhood*, New Brunswick, NJ: Rutgers University Press.

Frankel, S. (2012) *Children, Morality and Society*, Basingstoke, England: Palgrave Macmillan.

Gatto, J-T. (2005) Gatto, J. T. Dumbing us down: The hidden curriculum of compulsory schooling. New York, NY: New Society Publishers.

Gutman, L., Schoon, I. (2013) *The Impact of Non-cognitive Skills on Outcomes for Young People*, London, England: Education Endowment Fund and Institute of Education.

Hammond, S. A. (1998) *The Thin Book of Appreciative Enquiry,* Thin Book Publishing.

Hargreaves, D. (2004) *Learning for Life*, Bristol, England: Policy Press.

Hattie, J. (2009) *Visible Learning: a synthesis of meta-analysis relating to achievement*, London, England: Routledge.

Hattie, J. (2012). *Visible Learning for Teachers: maximizing impact on learning*. New York, NY; London, England: Routledge.

Hay Group, (2002) *Maverick: Breakthrough Leadership that Transforms Schools*, 1st ed. London, England: Hay Group Management Ltd.

James, A., James, A.L. (2004) *Constructing Childhood,* Basingstoke, England: Palgrave Macmillan.

James, A. Prout, A. (eds) (1997) [first published 1990] *Constructing and Reconstructing Childhood*, London, England: Falmer Press.

Jarvis, P., & Parker, S. (2005) *Human Learning: an holistic approach*, New York; London: Routledge.

Leckie, G., Pillinger, R., Jenkins, J. and Rasbash, J. (2010) *School, Family, Neighbourhood: which is most important to a child's education?* Research Briefing Paper 4 – retrieved from http://www.bris.ac.uk/media-library/sites/education/documents/research-briefings/research-briefing-04.pdf

Lucas, B. (2005) *Discover Your Hidden Talents,* London, England: Network Continuum Education Press

Mayall, B. (1994) 'Children in Action at Home and School' in B. Mayall (ed), *Children's Childhoods*, London, England: Falmer.

Matthews, P. Rea, S. Hill, R. & Gu, Q. (2014) *Freedom to Lead: a study of outstanding primary school leadership in England*, London, England: National College of Teaching and Learning.

McCulloch, G and Woodin, T (2010) Towards a social history of learners and learning', Oxford Review of Education, 36(2) 133-140.

IAPC (21/4/2016) (Institute for the advancement of Philosophy for Children) accessed 21/4/2016 http://www.montclair.edu/cehs/academics/centers-and-institutes/iapc/#d.en.9966

Pollard, A. (2014) *Reflective Teaching: in schools*, London, England: Bloomsbury.

Pollard, A. (1994) 'Towards a Sociology of Learning' in A. Pollard and J. Bounre (eds) *Teaching and Learning in the Primary School*, London: Rutledge.

Robinson, K. (2006) 'Do schools kill creativity?' retrieved from https://www.ted.com/talks/ken_robinson_says_schools_kill_creativity?language=en

Robinson, K. (2010) 'Bring on the learning revolution' retrieved from https://www.ted.com/talks/sir_ken_robinson_bring_on_the_revolution?language=en

Saint-Exupéry, A. d. (1943) *The Little Prince*, New York, NY: Harcourt, Brace & World.

Sarason, S. B. (1971) *The Culture of the School and the Problem of Change*, Boston, MA, Allyn and Bacon.

Spodek, B. and Saracho, O. (2013) *Handbook of Research on the Education of Young Children*, New York, NY: Routledge.

Stoll, L. and Bolam, R. (2005) 'Developing Leadership for Learning Communities', in M. Coles and G. Southworth (eds) *Developing*

Leadership: creating the schools of tomorrow, Maidenhead, England: Open University Press.

Stoll, L., Bolam, R., McMahon, A., Wallace, M., Thomas, S. (2006) 'Professional Learning Communities: a review of the literature' *Journal of Educational Change*, Volume 7, Issue 4, pp 221-258.

TLRP (Teaching and Learning Research Programme) (2007) 'Education, schooling and learning for life: how meaning and opportunity build from everyday relationships', *Teaching and Learning Research Briefing,* March 2007, No 23.

Watkins, C. (2005) 'Classrooms as Learning Communities: a review of research', *London Review of Education,* Vol 3, No 1 March 2005, 47-64.

Watkins, C. (2008) 'Depoliticisation, demoralisation and depersonalisation - and how to better them', *Pastoral Care in Education*, Vol26, No1, March 2005, 5-11.

Watkins, C. (2009) 'Learning about Learning', *School Leadership Today,* 1(3) 27-30.

Whitmore, J., Sir. (2009). *Coaching for Performance: GROWing human potential and purpose : The principles and practice of coaching and leadership* (4th ed.). London, England: Nicholas Brealey.

Woods, R. (2002) *Enchanted Heads: sustainability in primary headship*, National College for School Leadership.

Wrigley, J. Thompson, P., Lingrad, R. (eds) (2012) *Changing Schools,alternative ways to make a world of difference*, London, England: Routledge.

Yamashita, H., Davies, L. (2010) 'Students as Professionals' in B. Percy Smith and N. Thomas (Eds.) *A Handbook of Children and Young People's Participation,* London, England: Routledge.

United Nations Convention on the Rights of the Child (1989) - visit: http://www.ohchr.org/en/professionalinterest/pages/crc.aspx

Note:

For a comprehensive review of - *schooling* - see Pollard, A. (2014) *Reflective Teaching: in schools*, London, England: Bloomsbury.

For more on - *childhood studies* in general - see A. Corsaro, M.-S. Honig & J. Qvortrup (Eds.), *The Palgrave handbook of childhood* studies. Basingstoke, London: Palgrave Macmillan.

To understand more about *our theories and our view of the child* - see Frankel, S. (forthcoming) *Negotiating Childhoods: applying a moral filter to children's everyday lives*, Basingstoke, Enlgand: Palgrave Macmillan.